THE INTREPID GRINGO

THE INTREPID GRINGO

The true story of a fearless adventurer for God

Rosalie Hunt Mellor
Minita Sype Brown

Pacific Press® Publishing Association
Nampa, Idaho
Oshawa, Ontario, Canada
www.pacificpress.com

Book design by Eucaris L. Galicia
Cover photo provided by author

Unless otherwise marked, Scripture quotations are from the King James
Version of the Bible.

Library of Congress Cataloging-in-Publication Data

Mellor, Rosalie Hunt.
Intrepid Gringo: the story of a fearless adventurer for God/Rosalie Hunt
Mellor.
p.cm.
ISBN: 0-8163-2107-8
ISBN 13: 9780816321070
1. Sype, Ross. 2. Seventh-day Adventists—United States—Biography.
3. Missionaries—Central America—Biography. 4. Missionaries—West
Indies—Biography. 5. Missionaries—United States—Biography. I. Title.

BX6193.S96M45 2006
266'.67092—dc22
[B]
2005053514

Additional copies of this book are available by calling toll free
1-800-765-6955 or by visiting http://www.adventistbookcenter.com.

06 07 08 09 10 • 5 4 3 2 1

Dedication...

Affectionately dedicated
to the memory of Minita (Mickie) Sype Brown.

Contents

Preface

We have all thrilled to hear the exciting mission stories of Africa, Burma, China, and the Fiji Islands, perhaps not aware that our own pioneer missionaries just south of us in Central America and the West Indies were living equally exciting stories while bringing God's love to people lost in darkness. Today this area is a rapidly growing division in the denomination. If those pioneer workers could have looked into the future and seen the enormous harvest of those dedicated labors, they would have been truly amazed.

In 1918, Ross and Gertrude Sype went to Central America and the West Indies as missionaries. They were true pioneers, because at that time there were a few colporteurs and fewer pastors in that field. How impressed I was as a little girl when my exotic little cousin Minita Belle and her fascinating parents came home on furlough from the mission field. At those family reunions long ago, Uncle Ross, an enthusiastic, smiling man, told thrilling stories of hacking through jungle, riding in a dugout canoe across open waters, and suffering bouts of malaria. Not to be outdone, Aunt Gertrude, a commanding woman, had some pretty good stories of her own.

These are the experiences of this missionary family in the early twentieth century. It was a life of adventure filled with the joys of serving as well as the uncertainties, loneliness, sorrows, and dangers of working in uncharted and often hostile territory.

Years later Minita Belle, whom we later called Mickie, realized that when her parents were gone, the stories would go with them, so she was impressed to write a book and asked me to help her. Using Ross's memoirs and family letters as sources, we finished the manuscript and sent it off to the publishers. But the time was not right; missionary stories were not selling well twenty years ago. My copy went into my files, and one day in an unusual cleaning frenzy, I pitched it out. Mickie passed away, and I forgot about *The Intrepid Gringo* and went on to other things.

The manuscript has a story to tell of its own. Rejected, lost, thrown away, neglected, forgotten, stored in a place ransacked by thieves, it was found at last in a pile of rubble by a cousin of Ross's, Ann Gibson, and her husband, Larry Onsager. After Mickie died, the manuscript ended up in the hands of Ann's mother, Gertrude Gibson. Then after Gertrude died, Ann and Larry found it among her things, which had been stored, riffled through by thieves, and thrown on the floor. Ann picked it up and realized this was not only a piece of family history but church history as well. The survival of this manuscript has been a series of seeming coincidences, in the way it has been lost and found and finally reached the publisher, and even how Ann was able to find me, the surviving author.

Thanks go to a host of people along the way who have given a leg up. To Elders B. L. Archbold and Clayton Henriquez, both workers in the Inter-American Division for years, who took the time some twenty years ago to read the initial manuscript and offer suggestions. Also to Anna Hamlin for the letters from Ross, to Gertrude Gibson for hanging on to the manuscript through the years, to Ann Gibson for picking it up and taking it to Pacific Press, to Sula and Doug Lane and to Pam Talonen for moral support and technical help, and to the many who have helped me through the computer maze.

Chapter 1
The Hazelnut Party

The year 1898 was stamped forever in Ross's young mind as his first great year. In that year the Sype family moved from Iowa to a primitive mining camp in Wyoming, on the western frontier. The number eight came to be his magic number, and he dated the decades ending in eight (1898, 1908, 1918, and so on) as highly significant, charged with important events that brought changes in his life. Later he looked back on these years as the high watermarks in his long and adventurous life.

The Sype family, Logan and Minnie and three children, Ross, James, and Anna, were moving out west to a mining camp in Sheridan, Wyoming. The move took them from a staid, conservative farming community in southern Iowa, where life flowed on in peaceful monotony, to the raw, wild excitement of a mining camp.

James and Anna were not smitten by this move, but Ross caught a vision of a life of adventure and excitement. He had left the tranquil farm with no regrets and now sat at the window as the train swept through a land that changed from hour to hour and day to day, thrilling to see the West roll out before his eyes. All was new—the pronghorns bounding away, huge flocks of sheep, cowboys riding after herds of cattle, and at last the Rockies shouldering up in the distance, brooding and mysterious. For Ross, it was that moment in childhood when a door opens and lets in the future.

In Sheridan, Ross's father worked at the mines, taking care of the horses. His mother, with time on her hands and a burden on her heart, began giving Bible studies to the women in camp and was soon holding meetings and organizing Bible study groups. Her work progressed, and when the local conference officers saw the results, they gave Minnie a license to preach and to work as an evangelist on the frontier. Ross often drove his mother to her meetings because she had no sense of location.

When Ross was sixteen, Minnie got a call to go back to Iowa to hold evangelistic meetings, so the family returned to Iowa. That fall Ross enrolled in the Adventist academy at Stuart, Iowa. There he met Gertrude Hunt. He was not much given to poetry, but the first time he saw her he thought of a line from Byron: "She walks in beauty, like the night of cloudless clime and starry skies." He could never remember the rest of the poem, but those words went through his mind like a song whenever he saw her, and she became as that dark-haired vision clad in the qualities of ideal womanhood. She seemed to be at the center of every laughing group, always at the head of trooping students, a leader in serious discussions and high jinks as well. When she entered a room, no matter how dark and dreary the day, it was as if a light came on, and people looked up and began to smile and talk.

Ross watched Gertrude often from afar off, the tall, energetic figure moving as if there were not enough time for all she had to do. Her thick chestnut hair was piled up on her head in the style of the day, but he could not stop himself from wondering at the marvel of it if the pins were suddenly pulled out and shiny waves tumbled down her back and around her face. Confused by these thoughts, he could scarcely say hello whenever they met. Mumbling a greeting, he would slink by, leaving Gertrude to puzzle about this shy young man.

He felt a wide breach between her life and his, for she led out in prayer sessions and was always in church on Sabbath. Ross, on the other hand, was trying to shake off the rigid conformity of the church. He had decided to have as little to do with religion as possible. Although there were strict rules against it at Stuart Academy, he had started to smoke on the sly and was gradually moving in a direction away from the teaching of his boyhood. And all of this in spite of, or maybe because of, his mother's evangelistic work. Minnie's son was expected to be a paragon of virtue. Aware of his own temptations and ambitions, Ross found that this expectation threatened his autonomy, so he reacted by rebelling. His secret ambition at this time was to teach history in a worldly college. His dream was to travel to far-off, exotic places, have sophisticated friends and a fine collection of pipes, shake off the confines of the church, and live as he pleased.

The next year his brother, James, came to Stuart Academy. Unlike Ross, who was inclined to be a loner, James was friendly and outgoing and soon got swept up in the social life at school. The two boys roomed together. One evening the talk turned to girls, and after mentioning several who had caught his eye, James said with a great deal of enthusiasm, "Haven't you noticed that pretty Hunt girl from Ames?"

Ross looked steadily down at his boots and said that yes, he had noticed her. He had noticed the sun and the moon and the stars, too, he thought to himself, but that was all the good it did him.

"Well," James continued, "I'm going to make a bid for that young lady." He strode about the room very pleased with himself, while Ross wished desperately that his brother had never shown up on campus. "The guys voted her the prettiest girl in school, you know," James went on, smiling smugly at his reflection in the mirror as he passed it and patting at a stray lock of hair. "Yes, sir, the first chance I get . . ."

His chance came the next Sunday night at a get-acquainted party for the students. In spite of strict rules about the mixing of boys and girls, they were allowed to have partners for the games. James made a beeline for Gertrude and whisked her off. Ross watched covertly from the corner, trying to hide in the shadows as his brother courted the girl of his dreams. After that one game, however, James was seen with her no more. Later as the boys were going back to their room, Ross was curious and asked, "Say, little brother, you're supposed to be such a lady killer; what happened with the lovely Gertrude?"

"Oh, yeah, well, I tell you." James tried to laugh and shook his head ruefully. "I sort of misjudged her and, well—"

"Oh, I get it," Ross gleefully concluded for him. "You got too fresh, and she gave you the cold shoulder. Right?"

"Well, something like that." Always one to land on his feet, James brightened up immediately and, clapping Ross on the shoulder, exclaimed, "But say, kid, she is just the one for you. Go ahead; ask her to go with you sometime. I know you will like her."

"I know I will like her too, but—"

"But what? When is the next social?" James asked impatiently.

"I'm not sure," said Ross slowly, "but I think it's the hazelnut party in a couple of weeks."

"A hazelnut party!" James laughed. "What on earth is a hazelnut party?"

"The kids from the dorm go out to the timber and pick up hazelnuts," Ross explained. "It is sort of fun. They have a picnic and everything."

"Boys and girls?" James questioned. "Together?"

"Sure. You even get to choose a partner. But there is no slipping around. You know by now how the proctors have eyes in the back of their heads and ears like donkeys."

"You must ask Gertrude. What a good chance to really get acquainted out there in the timber, in spite of the proctors and their big ears."

"But what if she turns me down?"

"She won't if you get to her before someone else does. Go on, ask her," James urged.

"All right. I will," Ross replied with a determined edge to his voice.

He put it off for a week, and the time was drawing close, so one day after class he caught up with Gertrude and mustered enough nerve to ask, "Would you go to the hazelnut party with me?"

To his surprise she smiled warmly and replied, "I would love to go with you."

Too shocked to think of anything to say, Ross muttered a weak "Thank you" and turned and fled. It wasn't until much later that she confided to him that while all the other girls thought James was "cute" and "fun," her eye had been on his brother all along.

On that autumn day they walked side by side down the path leading to the bright woods, and there was a glow there that came not entirely from the clear sunny day. Squirrels chattered a warning, jays screamed "thief, thief," and the trees themselves seemed to laugh. It was more than chance that both young people reached for the same nut at the same time and that their hands seemed to touch ever so lightly. It was more than the brisk air that made cheeks flush and eyes sparkle. Nothing was said, but it was understood after that day that Gertrude was Ross's girl.

The week before Thanksgiving, Minnie Sype came to the academy to hold a revival with the students. There was quite a stir among the young people and a number were converted, but Ross was not among them. As Gertrude and many of Ross's friends went forward, he sat in stony silence. He did not want to hinder his mother's work, but neither did he feel motivated to surrender. He moved about the campus torn by the feelings within him, knowing he should yield to the pleadings of the Spirit but feeling some other force holding him back. He had reached an impasse in his spiritual life and could not move on.

Fall gave way to winter, and soon it was time for Christmas break. Ross went home for a few days, but because of his job, was back at the academy by New Year's Day. That evening was desolate and dreary, and except for a few other students and three teachers, the campus was virtually deserted. After work Ross walked to his room past the darkened buildings that huddled under a low gray sky. The wind gusted, blowing a scrap of paper across his path and into the ditch. Slouching along under rain mixed with snow, he pulled his collar up and shoved his hands deep into his pockets. There was a light in the dean's house, and seeing the family sitting in the warm living room as he shuffled past made him feel more lonely and cold than ever. He climbed the dark stairs to his room, pushed the door open and went in. He sat for a long time not lighting the lamp, not taking his coat off. The dorm had the strange unnatural silence of a place once happy and full but now emptied of all sound and life, as if it had died.

Sitting by himself in the gloomy room with his head in his hands, his thoughts turned to his own mortality and his place in the scheme of things. There that night the Holy Spirit spoke to Ross. Deeply moved by feelings he could not understand, he got up and, after lighting the lamp, found his Bible. It opened to Psalm 119, and the words of the ninth verse seemed to leap out at him. "Wherewithal shall a young man cleanse his way? by taking heed thereto according to thy word." It came like a voice from heaven. His resistance to the pleadings of the Spirit flashed through his mind—his choice of books and friends, the temptation he had with smoking. He sat there as if struck and read every verse down to the last. "I have gone astray like a lost sheep; seek thy servant; for I do not forget thy commandments." Never had anything impressed him with such power. Falling on his knees, he begged the Lord for forgiveness, and then taking *The Desire of Ages* from his bookshelf, he read far into the night. Much later, stiff and cold and tired, he arose to get ready for bed. Glancing at the calendar, he saw the date: January 1, 1908.

When Gertrude came back from vacation, they decided to "go steady." Ross thought back to the year 1898 when he had moved west with his family and found adventure, and now 1908, when he had found peace in his soul and a determination to serve the Lord, and found someone to share his life. He thought ahead to 1918 and wondered what might be in store for him.

Chapter 2
The Call

An aura of excitement surrounded Ross as he came up the walk to the house one spring morning in 1918. Jerking the door open, he burst into the house holding a sheaf of letters and papers. Puzzled, Gertrude watched as he nervously paced around the room, shuffled papers on the desk, sat down, got up. When he smiled, there was a telltale twitch around his mouth.

"What's up?" she asked.

"Nothing much. I've just been to the post office to get the mail. Here is a letter from your sister Georgia."

"Now I know a letter from my sister wouldn't get you all in a dither. What is so exciting?"

Then he drew out a long envelope and, handing it to her with a flourish, announced, "Here, my dear, is a letter from the General Conference that might interest you."

Gertrude took the letter and read it quickly. It was from the Mission Board—a call to Central America. She sat down and read the letter again before handing it back and saying lightly, "Central America, is it? So when do I pack?" But her voice sounded forced, and she could not keep the tears from welling up behind her eyes. Turning to look around the room, she saw it as unbelievably dear to her—the bright and shiny kitchen with the gold-banded plates on the yellow tablecloth, and the living room with the curtains she had made herself; the books; the pictures on the walls; the sofa her mother had given them when they got married. She felt her face sag with disappointment.

17

Seeing her so downcast, Ross took the letter and put it into his pocket, saying, "You don't want to go, do you? I understand you not wanting to leave your family and friends and our home. I'll wire the Mission Board and tell them we are unable to accept the call." Gertrude felt an immense sense of relief. She could stay here and be with people she knew and loved. Then she looked up and saw Ross with all of the joy gone out of his face, staring dully out of the window at the quiet street.

She spun around and took his hands, exclaiming, "Ross Sype, you'll do no such thing. You have wanted to work in the mission field all your life, and that is what you are going to do."

He folded her in his arms and kissed her tenderly, asking anxiously, "Are you sure you want to go? You like it here. This is your life."

"I'll like it there, too," she assured him. "I'll like it anywhere with you. We can come back to a safe and secure little church in the States later if we want to, but this is your chance for the career you want." She knew he had never been truly happy in small-town Iowa. Excitement and adventure were his life.

"The mission field has always been my first love," he said soberly. "I've dreamed about it all my life, serving God in some faraway place—New Guinea, the Ivory Coast, the Serengeti Plain . . ." His eyes took on a brooding quality as the rich names rolled over his tongue.

Gertrude smiled and patted his hand. "I know. I've known all along. But it has been so nice to have our own home. I guess I just settled down too much. Go on, send the wire saying you . . . no . . . we accept the call."

While Ross was gone she fixed lunch, making sandwiches and opening a jar of peaches. She felt a little sad as she heard the sounds of the town come in through the open window—the slow, comforting "clop, clop" of horses' hooves as a team plodded by drawing a wagon. From the yard a robin was singing very loudly above the noise of shouting children as they went past on their way back to school after lunch. Only that morning Gertrude had awakened as the sun was coming up and a rooster from a farm behind the house was crowing, shrill in the stillness. She knew how it stretched up on tiptoe, looking at the sun with eyes of gold, its comb like a crown. She had given a deep contented sigh before settling back to sleep, the covers of the bed holding her like arms.

After graduating from nursing school at the sanitarium in Nevada, Iowa, Gertrude had planned on a long career in nursing. However, when Ross became serious about entering the ministry and got a call from the Iowa Conference, he persuaded her he could not enter the work without her.

She had some misgivings about giving up a career she loved to marry a fledgling preacher, but love will have its way. They were married June 8, 1914, at her home church in Nevada, Iowa, in a double wedding ceremony with their friends Lineo and Evelyn Grandpre. The pastor who performed the ceremony was Elder L. C. Clemens, a cousin of Samuel Clemens, better known as Mark Twain.

Ross began his career as a helper in tent meetings. Their first home was a tent, and the address changed from week to week. The bride was truly challenged to prepare meals and keep her husband in clean white shirts.

In those innocent times of 1914 people flocked to lectures, traveling shows, circuses, and the Chautauqua and evangelistic meetings, where old-fashioned gospel was preached. Since Minnie Sype was also preaching in Iowa at that time, she and Ross held several meetings together. Crowds came from town and country in buggies, farm wagons, or on foot to hear this unique combination of mother and son. A few even drove cars, mostly Fords, but the one car remembered above all others was a Pierce-Arrow that drove up grandly but backfired as it pulled away, frightening the horses. After the meeting a flat tire brought the Pierce-Arrow to a limping halt before it had gone a full block. As he changed the tire, the driver who had arrived so proudly had to put up with the comments comparing horses to cars from people passing by.

The Lake City Seventh-day Adventist Church grew out of an evangelistic meeting held by Minnie and Ross Sype that resulted in a number of new converts. They had been holding regular services in various places, but as their numbers grew, they knew they must have a building of their own. They had decided to build a small church, but when they learned about a church building for sale out in the country, they decided to purchase it and move it to their lot.

The church that came to town caused quite a stir. Everyone turned out to watch it inch down the streets of Lake City. Muscled by men and horses, it was eased onto the lot prepared for it, where it stands to this day. In a few years after trees and shrubs had grown up, it seemed to have been there forever. Ross was called to be the first pastor of this church his mother had helped raise up.

Gertrude was happy to settle down at last, for while Ross thrived on the challenge of evangelism, she was beginning to tire of the constant moving, the new faces and places. When he was asked to pastor the church in Lake City, Iowa, he decided to settle down there more to please her than himself.

They worked hard to build up the infant church, which flourished under their leadership. When they moved into their very first house, Gertrude was able to give vent to her long buried homemaking instincts—fixing, sewing, and arranging. Most of all, though, she loved the stability of being in one place and having Ross come home every evening to the same house.

When Ross had returned from sending the wire to the General Conference, the two of them sat down to eat lunch. Gertrude asked, "Where are we going to live? I hope it isn't out in the jungle someplace in a little thatched hut up on stilts to keep the snakes and tigers from getting into the house."

Ross laughed and followed her gaze around the cozy little kitchen. "Oh, no, nothing like that," he assured her. "In fact, we will have our house in the Canal Zone in Panama, very cosmopolitan, a stopping-off place for missionaries on their way to other mission fields. So, my dear, you will entertain and be entertained, never fear."

"Well, that is a relief!" she sighed. "I don't mind learning Spanish or whatever they speak there, but I don't want to spend my time chattering to the monkeys in the trees."

"You know, Gertrude, we have been praying about our ministry," Ross said seriously, "and here is the call. I am sure it is God's will that we go to Central America." He took the envelope from the General Conference out of his pocket and turned it over, studying it with keen interest. "Nineteen-eighteen," he exclaimed. "Look, it's Nineteen-eighteen!"

"Yes, I know it is Nineteen-eighteen. What about it?"

Ross's face was radiant as he began to explain the significance of the year to Gertrude. "The decades ending in eight are special to me—always have been. Something invariably happens in those years to change my life. In Eighteen-ninety-eight I went out West and learned about adventure and a fuller life. In Nighteen-eight I became converted and in that year we became engaged. And now it's Nineteen-eighteen and we have the call to the mission field!"

Chapter 3
To the Mission Field

By July the young couple was ready for departure. Gertrude knew it was not going to be easy to say goodbye to her parents, especially her mother, who was never strong. She journeyed sadly to the old home in Nevada, Iowa, and slept that night in the big spare room, where the unsmiling portraits of ancestors looked down from the walls. The next morning she awoke to the smell of baking bread and knew that her mother, tiny and busy as a bantam hen in spite of her bouts with asthma, had gotten up early to make sweet rolls for breakfast.

Gertrude stood in the doorway of the old-fashioned kitchen with its round oak table, the old cook stove and kitchen cabinet, mixed with the very latest in modern design with its flour bin, round glass sugar bin, and porcelain counter, and she thought, *I'll remember this when I'm in the jungle with a tree stump and a camp fire.* Watching her mother taking rolls out of the oven, she had to fight back tears. "Oh, Mother, hot rolls!" she said, sitting down at the table. She buttered a crusty brown roll, not saying what was in her heart: *I hope you will stay well and I will see you again.* Instead she smiled and talked of other things while she ate, watching the butter melt into the roll and trying not to cry.

From the window she could see her father out by the barn hitching up the old horse to the wagon. For years he had collected discarded paper from some industry in town and stored it in the barn before shipping it out. The barn smelled of the baled paper, inky and faintly moldy. Years later in a crowded and noisy street in Nassau, Bahamas, Gertrude caught a whiff of the same moldy paper smell, and as she cast about for the origin, the memories came flooding back of her father hitching up the white horse and driving off that morning. He was a huge vision of a man, who with his head of unruly white hair looked like an Old Testament prophet. Never employed at a regular job, he worked as a drayman and somehow managed to eke out a living hauling goods for people and selling the baled paper stored in the barn. He considered his real job to be bringing what he called "the truth" to his neighbors and family. Gertrude and her brothers and sisters learned early in life to hustle for themselves. Their childhood provided few luxuries but developed in them a fierce independence and survival instinct.

Ross and Gertrude took the train from the small Iowa town where Ross's mother had come to see them off. His father had earlier gone out West seeking a suitable climate for an asthmatic condition that plagued him. Anna had married and moved away, and James had been tragically killed while still a young man. Minnie would be left quite alone, with nothing to sustain her but God's love and her work. She watched the train pull away, and Ross and Gertrude waved until she was only a dot standing beside the bleak little station.

Ross and Gertrude took a small boat from Miami, the first time either had been on the ocean. They soon found out that while Ross was an excellent sailor, Gertrude was nauseated, and she hung over the rail with other seasick landlubbers. As the boat approached Cristóbal, Canal Zone, Ross saw for the first time the place he had dreamed about so often. Spread before him was that land of blue and green and the stark white beaches, the intense colors in the bright hard sunshine, and in the streets a mingling of many peoples walking slowly or sitting in the shade of the broad-leafed trees. He felt in some strange way that he had come home. The smell of ginger and jasmine seemed familiar, as did the sound of parrots screaming and the sudden flight of a flock of parakeets, blue against the green foliage. But it was the coconut palms that truly set the stage for the tropics—so unlike trees in the north. They grew very tall and held aloft the green fruit shaped like giant footballs. They were everywhere, languid in the heat, swaying slightly, the leaves unbelievably long. He smiled at Gertrude. He felt as if at last he was where he belonged.

Ross didn't even seem to mind the steaming heat, for he had always liked warm weather, saying the hotter it got the better he felt. Gertrude, on the contrary, was miserable in the hot steamy air and made a futile effort to cool herself with a small fan. "Ross," she gasped, "I just can't take this heat. It is unbearable."

Ross's answer was hardly consoling. "I think this is the hottest part of the day. The late afternoons and the evenings are cooled by the trade winds, and the mornings aren't too bad." Then waving and pointing he shouted, "Well, look who's here!" There to meet them were old friends of academy days, Roy and Gussie Bowles. Roy worked for the Pacific Press Publishing Company in the Canal Zone. Learning that Ross and Gertrude were coming, they met the boat, eager to see someone from home.

After much laughing and hugging and excited talking, Gertrude asked, "How did you know we would be on this boat?"

"We have the most efficient grapevine in the world here," Roy answered. Then picking up the two suitcases he shouted, "Follow me," and he and Gussie led them across the busy, noisy street. "Now we are going to get you a Caribbean taxi called a *cochero,*" he explained as a one-horse vehicle drew up. Giving the driver an address, they threw the luggage aboard and all piled in.

"Well, I never . . ." Gertrude looked at the horse and then at Roy and Gussie and asked, "Can that skinny little pony pull all of us and our bags too?"

"Have no fear," Roy said with a laugh. "They may not be as big as your draft horses back in Iowa, but they are wiry and strong and could pull us all day."

The *cochero* wound its way along the narrow, teeming streets between buildings, squalid and close set for the most part, made of wood and corrugated iron. Here and there a few new structures had been built and were a sharp contrast to the old buildings. Every conceivable type of vehicle and draft animal was moving along those streets. Ross and Gertrude couldn't help staring at the street scene, so different from the well-ordered streets in Iowa.

"Not like back home, is it," Gussie remarked. "Imagine what a riot that ox cart would cause on the main streets of Lake City, Iowa."

The ox cart rumbled past, solid wooden wheels moving ponderously. Light-stepping donkeys walked in and out of the traffic carrying bulging burdens. Vendors hawked their wares, and women in bright clothes balanced huge loads of produce on their heads, moving with a sensuous grace, padding along barefooted.

"How do they do it?" Gertrude asked, turning to Roy and Gussie. "How do they balance those loads on their heads?" Then she saw one that made her gasp. "Why, look there! There is a woman carrying a trussed-up pig. Why, it is alive! I saw it move!"

She almost forgot the heat in watching this panorama before her. She was so quick moving she couldn't help but notice the lackadaisical way everybody was sauntering along, in no hurry to get anyplace. Everything and everyone moved at this relaxed pace, the people, the oxen, the donkeys, and their own *cochero.* She watched the leisurely flow of traffic for a while and then blurted out, "Look how slow everyone moves! You'd think they had all day to get wherever they're going."

"Never mind, Gertrude," Roy answered with a knowing smile. "You'll slow down too. The constant heat, you know. It really takes the starch out of you after a while."

Later, after they had freshened up in their small temporary quarters and eaten dinner, a little breeze began to blow, bringing relief from the torrid heat. As the shadows lengthened and the sun grew less intense, they thought they would enjoy the cool twilight and were surprised when darkness came suddenly, like turning off a light. "Not even twilight," Gertrude commented as she lit the lamps. "Folks back home will have trouble believing all this."

But she was talking to herself as Ross, like someone in a dream, paced around the room muttering to himself. "Look here," he said suddenly. "Just look at this." And he pinned a map on the wall, marking it with a pencil as he talked. "This is our field—Venezuela, Colombia, Panama, Costa Rica, Nicaragua, and two island groups: the Columbian Islands, two hundred and fifty miles out in the Caribbean from Panama, and the Corn Islands off the coast of Nicaragua." He stepped back to look at the map. The checks he had made were tiny dots in the huge blue Caribbean Sea. "And think of this. In that vast territory our church has no more than five ministers and a few colporteurs."

Gertrude studied the map and then asked, "Will you be doing evangelism then?"

"Elder Spicer seemed to think so, but Roy told me they are so short of pastors that he wouldn't be surprised if I'd end up pastoring a group of churches either here or in Bocas del Toro farther up the coast. Elder Kneeland, the president, is away visiting some of the outlying churches, so we'll have to wait until he returns before we know."

"I hope it isn't Bocas del Toro. That sounds so far away from everything. I like to be where there are people to talk to. You don't think he'll send us there, do you?" asked Gertrude with more than a little concern.

"I really don't know. It is a main port—a shipping center and in a good location on the Chiriqui Lagoon, so he may want us there. Did you know that city is named after the inlet from the ocean to the lagoon? Bocas del Toro means 'mouths of the bull'!"

"Romantic sounding, but from what I have heard I hope we don't have to live there."

Secretly Ross also hoped that would not be their fate, although rumor had it that Elder Kneeland wanted to establish a church in that location. Ross had heard things about that little port that made him want to avoid going there at all costs. Flat, humid, and mosquito ridden, it was called the pest hole of Central America because of the many deaths from malaria and black water fever. Two workers were already buried there, and he had little interest in joining them.

Chapter 4
Letters From Panama

Cristóbal, Canal Zone, Panama
July 30, 1918

Dear Folks at Home,

Well, as we are at our journey's end and have been here for nearly a week and have begun to see how people live and learn their customs, I will tell you something of the place and what we have already seen. We get our mail at the Cristóbal post office as we told you before we left, but we live in the native city of Colón, which is really only separated from Cristóbal by the railway tracks. We live in the section of Colón which is only for white people, and I assure you it is not a very large section, as this town has a population of about fifty thousand of every nation under heaven (almost). There are many Chinese merchants and saloonkeepers—some of the leading merchants and wholesalers are Chinese. I would like to repeat to you some of the names of these merchants, "Wung Chung Wo & Co." Etc., etc.

And then there are many Malaysians who are merchants. They wear their turbans like they do in India and the Malay country . . . if you get into their stores it is a pretty hard thing to get out without buying, and then there are hundreds of native people who run little one-horse stores—dirty looking places that you would not care to buy at. But some of these Malay stores are very fine. Most of the population is Negroes; some of them are from Haiti and speak French; some of them are native and speak Spanish; some of them speak all three; and some speak such a jumble of a language that hardly anyone can understand them. I think there are more of them that speak English and Spanish than any of the other.

Of course the native Panamanians are mostly a mixture of Spanish and Indian. These people are not very many here at Colón, but over at Panama City you see more of them and more of the real Indian than here. However, there are quite a few of both of them here. We see a few of the San Blas Indians where white people are not allowed. They come here to sell their pineapples and bananas.

We are wonderfully surprised at the health conditions here on the Zone and in Colón and Panama City. The United States has complete control of sanitary conditions in these two cities as well as on the Zone. We have not seen a mosquito nor a fly since we have been here, which is nearly a week. They have made it mighty uncomfortable for the mosquitoes, and it is a wonderful thing when you think that before Uncle Sam took hold of things that they almost ate people up and sickness was so bad that it was a very usual thing for twenty-five people to die every day. Now it is almost what you would call a health resort, for death rate is very small. They have accomplished this great change by draining all the swamps close by and by paving these towns and fixing complete drainage and sewage systems; and then, where there is a low spot that is vacant, they spray it with something that makes it very unhealthful for the mosquitoes.

It is not nearly so hot as we expected. We suffer but little from heat. However, we sweat very easily. Can't keep powder on very well. The only way to really keep feeling good is to take a good cold spray every morning. This is a great thing and invigorates you and makes you feel fine. . . .

It rains here very often this time of year. I understand that the rain begins in April . . . and in September gets worse through October and most of November and then the dry spell begins in December and gradually gets dryer and warmer for January, February, and March. . . .

It is during those dry months that they hold their tent meetings . . . so you see, when you are suffering with the cold we will be holding tent meetings.

The morality here among these natives is very low. Virtue is very scarce. Many are great tobacco fiends. The women go around with long homemade cigars in their mouths, smoking as big as you please . . . good-sized children run down the street as naked as the day they were born. And the children are as thick as the hair on your head. Many of these large families live in one little room. In fact, most of them do. It would be impossible for Americans to live in these native quarters. A building is just like a beehive. Every room has a family in it. Some buildings house twenty-five or thirty of these big families and the buildings are not big either.

Another brother and myself visited in this district a while this afternoon. We visited one young lady who is living the truth in just such a place as this. . . . It is wonderful what this truth is doing for these natives.

Last Sabbath I should have liked for you to have been to church with us. We have a membership of over one hundred, nearly all of them black. . . . And they are so orderly that it would put many of our churches in Iowa to shame. And they know their lesson. The class that I went in to had a big black teacher (as all the rest did), and I tell you they are better teachers than most of the Sabbath School teachers at home.

We are now building a fine new $5,000 church building. . . . It will be the best church in Colón. Last Sunday night I gave my initiatory sermon to about two hundred black natives. I tell you it was a new experience. But they all seemed to appreciate it very much.

Now I am going to tell you about some of the native customs. They have little native cabs which I cannot describe but will try to send you a picture of them sometime. When you want one of them you just clap your hands and one of them will come a running. They drive a little mule or else a pony. They take you as far as you want to go for ten cents American money.

1918

Yesterday as I was walking down a street here in Colón I thought, "I wish the folks could have a picture of me and my surroundings." I was visiting in one of the native narrow streets; not a white man in sight except myself. The narrow street was swarming with black people, naked children running along the street, and women in bare feet carrying loads on their heads and other sights otherwise too numerous to mention. As I passed through the throng they looked at me and wondered what I was doing in their midst. Really, it was interesting.

November 2, 1918

This afternoon we had a memorial service for a brother who died in Jamaica. He was a member here and his wife is here. It was a sad case. Last spring they went to Jamaica on account of his health, but they are poor West Indian people and she wanted to work to support them as he was not able. There was scarcely any work in Jamaica, and what there was, the wages were so small she couldn't meet expenses. So she left him there and came back here to Colón where she could get more for her work. She is one of our best members. For a couple of months now the steamship service has been almost cut off with Jamaica so we have had no mail from there for nearly that long until yesterday a ship came in and brought a letter stating that this brother had died over a month ago. Just think how it would seem to know your husband had been dead and buried a month before you knew anything about it. On account of poor steamship service the money she had sent him had not reached him, so he died in the poorhouse. Well, these sad things happen right along here in these fields where travel is difficult and mail communication is poor.

December 1918

It is surely interesting to deal with these people. They are such odd people. One must learn to love them and be patient and lead them, but not try to drive them, and some must be carried. I am trying to show them all that I love them, and they seem to appreciate it so much. They have not always been treated just right by the white people. I always try to pay lots of attention to them. When one deals right with them they will do anything to please him. It surely trains a person to be a shepherd.

Christmas 1918

Well, we have had a hard time realizing that this is Christmas time. We did not need any speculations as to whether it would be a white Christmas as well. We just felt like it must be the Fourth of July instead of Christmas. All the workers met at the Bowleses' and ate our dinner together.

All of us mentioned the fact that it hardly seemed possible that it was really that time of year for we were eating in a house with no plaster, no window glass—just as open as it could be and we were plenty warm. We would not have had to go very far to have found some children with no clothes on at all.

There must have been some storms up in the States somewhere a couple weeks ago for there were bad storms on the water. They had what they call a "norther." We could see the waves beating away up over the break water that protects the harbor here. Our conference president and conference treasurer were out in the storm in a little sailing vessel. The storm tore the sails off and then broke the rudder and left them to drift on the mighty waves of the great deep. They drifted for ten days, and then as they were about out of food and water they landed on the coast of Panama about twenty miles below here. There a U.S. submarine chaser picked them up and brought them home. They started from here for the island of St. Andrews to visit the brethren there. It was expected that they would be about a day and a half on the trip, but they were caught in the norther. Instead of reaching St. Andrews they drifted past the coast of Nicaragua and then drifted east and finally saw that if they were not stopped in some way the current was going to carry them to the coast of South America. They finally sighted land and drifted close enough to see where they were. . . . The chaser came along and picked them up.

When they got home they looked very much worse for the wear. This gives you some idea of the vicissitudes of travel in our conference. It isn't as much pleasure as it is in some places. In such situations as that a person can sympathize a little with Paul, and one learns to depend on the power of God. The captain of the boat, though rough, acknowledged that it was only by the grace of God that they were alive. That little boat would ride away to the top of a mighty wave higher than a high building and then it would dart down to the bottom of the wave in a valley between waves, and one would think that they were to be swallowed up, but the boat would come up to the top of the wave again and thus they drifted in that storm.

These people carry everything on their heads. They even carry the mail home from the post office on their heads. Last night Gertrude gave Jane a dish of ice cream to take home to her girl, and she walked off with it on her head, just balanced there as if it were glued. It looked so funny that we all had to watch her as she walked down the street.

The native women carry everything on their heads. They don't hold on at all. They just balance them. The other day one of them was going down the street with a great heavy load on her head, and a dog came out barking. She kicked at the dog, but kept her load perfectly balanced as if it were glued to her head. . . .

I started this letter several days ago but as there was no boat leaving for the States I have not hurried it. Mail is very slow. We have been here a week and a half and today was the first time we have heard a word from home. . . . Not a scratch from mother nor Gertrude's folks, although I am sure they wrote and will reach us by and by, but if mail goes by New York it takes so long. Some of the letters had been on the way over three weeks. Anna's letter had been opened by the censor. Most mail goes through the censor now days on account of the war. I see by today's paper that the Germans are on the run. We have a good daily paper here.

Georgia said in her letter that bananas were five cents apiece there and not good ones either. We pay eight cents per dozen here for good ones and can get them as cheap as thirty-five cents or so for a whole bunch. . . .

I will tell you next time about my trip to Panama City and Ancon and Balboa. These towns are all at the other end of the Canal. I would like to send you pictures of the Canal, but we are not allowed to send any pictures of the Canal during the war.

I will not write more for this time. I expect you will be at camp meeting by the time this arrives.

With love,
Ross

February 26, 1919
Colony of New Providence, R.P.

Well, I am in exile sure enough now. I am holding a series of meetings out here in the jungles in the colony of New Providence. Some place! You say "Goodbye" to everything when you come out here—no telephones, no post offices, no electric light, no anything. It is sure a lonesome place. All through the day the men are gone to the mountain to work on their "farms." Yesterday I crossed the lake early in the morning and reached Monte Lirio, Canal Zone, in time to take a morning train to Colón and spent the day at home and came back for evening service.

We're having a good attendance and a good interest in our meetings. A few years ago they had an apostasy in the Adventist church here on the Isthmus and a large number of these West Indian Adventists separated and formed a new church called "The Ethiopian Association of Seventh-day Adventists." They made their headquarters here in this colony and built a church. Gradually they have come back to the church until they only have eight members left, and I am trying my best to get them all back and then the organization will be broken up. I have succeeded in getting the most intelligent one back. Last night he came and requested to unite with us again. He is a fine fellow. I hope by the Lord's help to get them back before I leave here.

I am using my stereopticon out here and these people seem to enjoy it very much. I am getting a lot of stereopticon slides made of this country so when we come back to the States we can show some of the interesting things here.

Panama City, R.P.

February 17, 1920

We have been having much excitement here this week. It is Carnival Week. This is nothing like what we call carnivals in the States. It is connected with the Catholic fiesta (feast) of Mardi Gras. They surely do carry on! You see, Mardi Gras comes just before Lent so they can expel all their surplus energy and then settle down to being "good" during Lent. They all dress in all kinds of ridiculous costumes and wear masks, etc. They then drive up and down the main street yelling and screaming silly songs in Spanish. Then some fellows run up and down the street fixed up like devils with horns and hoofs and tails and carry forks in their hands and run at people. Others dress like—well, like every imaginable and unimaginable creatures. They throw bushels of confetti and serpentines, and squirt some liquid stuff in everyone's faces. They have a queen of the carnival who rides in a magnificent wagon fixed with a throne with many seats for her ladies of honor, while she sits high on a beautiful throne, and as the people wave and clap she throws kisses to them.

We had a great treat last week. A good visit with Elder Charles Thompson and two other General Conference men. Elder Thompson stayed one night with us and preached in the Panama church.

We are beginning a campaign now to raise money for a new church in Panama City. The General Conference has promised to give us $3,500.00 if we raise that much, so we are going after it.

April 20, 1920
Dear Mother,

Elder Trummer is very nice to me. He told me he was learning lots from my way of dealing with these people. They all think I have succeeded to a remarkable degree in adapting myself and learning how to handle them. If it were not for that, I guess I could more easily leave [Evidently, she was encouraging him to try to get a call back to the States.], but they have many difficulties in finding people who can adapt, and when they do find one, they hate to see them go. The church at Colón acted so glad to see us. They say they can't love anyone like they do Elder and Mrs. Sype, although they think Elder Trummer a lovable man and all think much of him.

Everyone has their strong points and weak ones. My strong point seems to be in winning the affections of these people, but I wish I could accomplish some other of the great problems just as well as I do that one. Some other things perplex me much. It is quite a task to manage two large churches and especially so when dealing with different ethnicities. It takes continual study. I remember what you said once about those who take up home missionary work in conferences. You said they should have had the practical experiences that come in pastoral work. I guess I am getting some of those experiences.

I saw General Pershing today. He is visiting the Canal Zone inspecting the fortifications, etc. He is a very pleasant-appearing man. I was glad to get the chance of seeing him.

May 31, 1920
Dear Pearl, Anna, and Children,

This is some fun trying to write with the train going at a good hickory and swinging us around the corners. I am on my way to the city of Colón again. It seems like I have to get back over there every little while. Gertrude went over yesterday to do some sewing. She will be leaving in just nine days (for the States) and "poor me" will be a bachelor. But believe me, I will be anxious for two months to pass by for then I, too, will be (just went through a tunnel) sailing away to the U.S.A., the Lord willing.

We feel much encouraged as to the results of our Hall meetings. Last night ten new souls came forward to take their stand for God and His message; and many arose for prayer. We have secured many names of cognizant people who are interested and want literature. By the Lord's help we hope to do much good in following up the work of the meetings.

We are now passing a canal lock, and a big ocean steamer is going into the lock to be lowered down to the next level toward the Pacific Ocean.

We surely have a large problem on our hands now to raise about $11,000.00 to buy a lot and build a church. We do need it so badly. We are working hard to get it, but these people are so poor. There is not a single member of the Panama church who has an income of more than $50.00 per month, and most of them have less. One sister supports a family of four on $16.00 per month, and there are others who get just as little and even less. Then consider that things are just as high here as in the States if they were to live the same way, but they don't. They eat simple native food and live in little cramped quarters in a way that no American could live. I hardly see how some of them exist (they don't live).

We are now gliding along by the side of the Canal and I can see two steamers, one headed toward the Atlantic, the other to the Pacific, and they will soon pass each other. One is flying the American flag; the other, the English flag. The American ship is headed toward the Atlantic and has probably been to the west coast of South America and bound for New York. The English ship is probably bound for the west coast of South America. It is very interesting to see these ships of all nations going through the Canal. You would be surprised to know how much it costs a large steamer to get the privilege of going through the Canal. A real large steamer may pay as much as $15,000.00. Most of them pay about $5,000.00. Even at that rate they save thousands of dollars as well as much time by not going away around the south points of South America as they used to do. I believe it is a dollar per ton. The year 1919 was a big year in Canal traffic. There was almost a steady stream of ships going through the Canal at times. It is sure a great thing.

Panama City, R.P.

March 8, 1921

We are moving back to Colón the last of this month. Gertrude is surely glad of that as she has never cared for Panama City. We will live in the new mission home, which was purchased while we were in the States. . . .

About the war that is going on here between Panama and Costa Rica— we are having all kinds of excitement. Among other things, there is quite an anti-American feeling among the natives because the United States sent American troops into Panama to protect the Panamanian president from the fury of the mobs, and also because the U.S. tells them that they must settle the trouble at once and stop their scrapping. They don't seem to realize that if it were not for the U.S., Costa Rica could come in and eat them alive, for Panama has no guns nor ammunition to speak of at all and are just sending mobs.

Chapter 5
Into the Jungle

Ross's fears about Bocas del Toro nearly became a reality, for when Elder Kneeland returned and called the conference committee together, it was clear from the beginning that he intended to send Ross and Gertrude there. It seemed to be a pet project of his, and he talked at great length of the need there and the potential of the place. He was so persuasive that if Ross hadn't been previously warned, he would have thought it was opportunity knocking.

However, almost every worker he had met since coming to the Isthmus had pictured the horrors of that place to him—the squalor, the heat, the isolation and loneliness, not to mention the mosquitoes and the diseases they carried. He himself, always fascinated by an unusual challenge, was intrigued rather than appalled, but Gertrude—what would he tell her? What about his promise that they would be living on the Isthmus, where she would have the companionship of other workers? She needed people, activity, something to do. She liked to make things happen, not vegetate in some backwater place, no matter how exotic.

When Ross met with the committee at last, it moved ponderously as committees do. He was on pins and needles while Elder Kneeland made his pitch to send the young missionaries to Bocas del Toro. This was discussed from every angle, and at last one of the men spoke up. "Actually, Elder, I feel we need a pastor on the Isthmus. After all, there are eight churches here and much more opportunity for evangelism than at Bocas."

This turned the tide, and then all spoke in favor of it and were nodding in agreement. Cecil Dutcher, conference secretary, said enthusiastically, "People

36

are more receptive here. It seems to me it would be a great waste to send Elder Sype off to Bocas while eight churches languish right here for want of leadership."

As the talk went back and forth, Elder Kneeland began to agree until at length he turned to Ross and asked, "Well, Elder, how would you like to be the pastor on the Isthmus?"

Relief flooded over Ross, and he shook hands with the committee members and hurried home with the good news. On the way he stopped to buy a mango as a way of celebrating his new post. When he came in the door he shouted in great glee, "Shake hands with the new pastor on the Isthmus!"

"I'll do better than that. How will a kiss do? Oh, Ross, I was so worried they would send us to Bocas del Toro. Gussie told me they might, and she said it was a terrible place. People have died there of malaria and black water fever, workers like us. I didn't want to tell you."

Ross nodded his head. "I know. Roy told me the same thing, and I didn't want to tell you, but that is behind us now. Look at what I brought you. I know how you love fruit."

"What is it?"

"This, my darling, is one of the most exotic fruits in the tropics," he said, holding it up dramatically.

"That funny looking little melon is exotic?"

She took it in her hand, looked at it this way and that, and asked, "How do you eat it?"

"Cut it up, I guess. They say it is best eaten in the bathtub, so it is probably messy." They cut it open, laughing like children as the juice ran over hands, faces, and mouths. Gertrude couldn't decide whether it tasted like pears and apricots; or melon and pineapple; or peaches, melon, and banana; but Ross, still jubilant over his new position exclaimed, "It tastes of the tropics, of the trade winds, of the sun, mysterious, tantalizing . . ."

Gertrude brought him back to earth by reminding him that if they were going to be residents there, they had better be looking for a house, so after washing the mango juice from faces and hands, they set forth. After much walking and looking they found an apartment for rent a few blocks from the Colón church. Moving in and getting settled was not a hard task because they had accumulated very little of this world's goods. When they had worship that evening, they thanked God for their new home and for all of His blessings, not forgetting to mention their thankfulness for being in Colón and not in Bocas del Toro.

The next morning Gertrude heard the familiar crowing of a rooster, clear and far away. The innocent notes announcing a new day broke against her ear as she lay in that twilight zone between sleeping and waking. Thinking she was back home, she expected to hear the milkman's horse and the rattle of bottles on the porch, but the peaceful moment was shattered by a high, wild scream that ended in a choking gurgle. Suddenly wide awake, she sat up in bed and shook her sleeping husband. "Ross, Ross, wake up," she hissed, "someone is being murdered."

He rolled over and rose up on one elbow, listening. The scream came again, violent and savage in the morning stillness. Patting her hand, he smiled and said, "Relax. It's only the peacocks waking up. They keep them as pets around here. Not like the meadowlarks back home, hey?"

"Oh," she almost sobbed. "I was dreaming we were back in our room in Lake City. I heard a rooster like I used to from the farm behind the house. I really did hear a rooster, and then that . . . that . . ."

Ross, who was wide awake now, looked at the clock and leaped to his feet, exclaiming, "Oh, I say, this is the day Jacob is coming to take me to visit some of my jungle churches! He wanted to get an early start before the heat of the day." He began to dash around getting ready, for this was to be his first excursion into the bush, and he was tremendously excited. Gertrude could not share his enthusiasm as he flung things around, trying to decide what to wear. Glancing up and seeing her forlorn face, he came to her and took her hand and said consolingly, "Cheer up, dear. I know there are a lot of new things, and it will take time to get used to it all." She got up then and began to prepare breakfast, and when Jacob Osborne, the publishing secretary, arrived, she had regained her usual good humor and they were all able to laugh about the rude awakening at dawn.

Chapter 6
Bush Church

The first church Ross and Jacob were going to visit was the Pueblo Nuevo church. The path the two men took tunneled through a green tangle of vines and trees growing close on either side, shutting out the sun. In 1918 those jungles were a paradise for animals and birds, and Ross was overwhelmed by their variety and numbers. Wonderful flocks of birds fled before them; uncounted birds, brilliant and iridescent, screamed at the intruders. Monkeys swung through the trees high above them, and tropical flowers, gaudy and theatrical, grew out of reach. Although it was hot and humid as they worked their way up the path, Ross was oblivious to the discomfort, being aware only of this magic place of bright colors set against the green and tangled background, where leaves grew to undreamed-of sizes and shapes and where any vine might turn into a snake before your eyes.

They came at last to a clearing where the underbrush and trees had been hacked away. Ross, almost in a trance, was brought back to reality by Jacob's announcement. "Here we are, first stop—the Pueblo Nuevo church."

"What?" Ross exclaimed, focusing on the simple native hut. "You mean this is it? This is the church?"

"This is it," Jacob insisted with a broad smile. "What did you expect?"

"Well, not Westminster Abbey, but not exactly this either," Ross said, walking around the building, still not willing to believe his eyes as he studied the thatched-roof structure, built up on stilts against the ravages of the jungle. It boasted one door, and the windows were open to the elements and the insects.

Beside the church was a smaller building that Jacob explained was for the pastor to stay in when he was visiting in the area. No other houses were in sight—no village, no hut, nothing but the oppressive, brooding silence of the close-growing trees all around. It was very still and hot as the sun beat down from overhead. Unfamiliar trees ringed the clearing, and one in particular caught Ross's attention. "What kind of tree is that over on the other side with the long pods hanging from it?" he asked.

"Those aren't pods; they are monkeys," Jacob answered. "Watch!" He clapped his hands and shouted, and the tree came to life. Ross watched in fascination as gray, long-tailed monkeys jumped from one limb to another, hanging by their tails and chattering at the earthbound men standing below looking up at them.

When the men entered the church, they heard a dry rustling sound as some creature scurried away, but the building was swept clean, and crude benches were lined up on either side. Jacob nodded in approval and said, "Looks as if they have been here sweeping up. They are expecting us. Got your sermon ready, Elder?"

"Yes, but I don't expect there will be many here."

"Don't be too sure. The word is out all over the jungle." Jacob stepped to the door and seemed to be listening for something. Then from out of the deep, palpable silence around them Ross heard it, a distant sound like singing. Slowly it grew louder until he could hear it plainly, human voices singing a hymn. The familiar melody came to him clearly now. "On a hill far away stood an old rugged cross . . ." When he went to the door and looked out, Ross could see a procession of people winding toward them out of the dense jungle. The singing was louder now and more joyful, with men's and women's voices harmonizing as they sang the sweet hymn.

They were barefoot, dressed in their best, and overjoyed because a pastor had come to preach. Ross felt humbled as he stood before those radiant, up-turned faces and felt the longing in their hearts for the gospel message. His own cup was filled to overflowing as he preached in that simple church. After the service, the church brothers and sisters shook hands all around and departed as they had come, walking barefoot up the path, melting into the dark jungle, singing as they went.

That night the missionaries stayed in the primitive hut reserved for visiting ministers, and Ross never forgot his first night in the jungle. In the black night, in a frail little wooden shelter, how great the majesty of God seemed to him. He awoke once and listened briefly to the strange night sounds. Looking out of the open window, he saw the Southern Cross in the sky and knew he was where he belonged. This land appealed to the very fibers of his being, and he went to sleep content.

From then on, visiting the bush churches never failed to charm and interest Ross. Some were so primitive and out of the way they made the Pueblo Nuevo church seem almost modern in comparison. Since this was before the widespread use of the automobile, getting to the churches was an adventure in itself. Public transportation was haphazard at best. Trains, boats, and ox or horse-drawn carts came and went seemingly at will, for there was no timetable. Making connections was largely a matter of luck.

The brethren at Colón wished the young missionary God-speed as he set forth one warm morning on the first leg of a journey by train across the Isthmus to Gatun Lake. The train moved along the bank of the lake for several miles and then ran out over a peninsula, where it stopped at a lonely station and Ross got off. He stood on the platform watching the train disappear without him and feeling as if he were at the end of nowhere. The first of the churches, with the promising name of New Providence, was in a scattered settlement far out in the jungle. The membership, while not large, was able to support a neat little native church.

The rest of the journey was to be by boat, and Ross had to inquire which one was going to New Providence as there were many boats moored there waiting like taxis to meet the train. All the other passengers were natives, mostly women carrying large baskets on their heads, who had gone to Gatun and Colón on this Friday to sell vegetables and buy supplies. They handled the huge loads with a great deal of skill and had splendid balance. One poor old grandmother caught Ross's attention as she struggled with a large bundle in her hands and, in addition, a big basket on her head. She was clearly unable to lift the parcel onto the boat. Seeing her dilemma, Ross went to her aid. Her grateful smile showed her thanks, and after the boat had taken them across to the other side, and the passengers had picked up their packages, disembarked, and walked off in all directions, she stopped to thank him again.

Ross started walking in what he hoped was the right direction, and after a mile or so began to see houses and small pineapple fields. Before long he was met along the trail by the local elder coming out to find him. He took Ross to his small house, of which he was very proud, as it was a little better than average, having a spare room for the pastor.

The next day, Sabbath, the congregation came, some walking and others by boat, among them the old woman Ross had helped on the trip over. She did not belong to the church, but upon learning that her benefactor was a minister, she wanted to hear the preaching of the man who had helped a stranger.

Up the Chagress River from New Providence was a church even more remote and primitive than this one. Ross went there for the first time on a Friday and stayed in a little hut connected to the church. When he entered the room that night it was already dark, and he heard a sinister stirring up in the thatch as if it was inhabited by a huge object. Knowing it might be a large snake, he slept fitfully and was glad to see the sun come up in the morning. What Ross remembered most about that church was the conch shell blown by the elder. Since the elder was the only one who had a watch, he came to church early every Sabbath, and one hour before time for services he would blow a conch shell. The sound carried for miles, and when the people heard this primitive church bell, they began the journey to church over beaten trails or across waterways. Years later when Ross had forgotten the name of the elder and of the church, he remembered vividly the creepy rustle in the thatch above his head and, in the morning, the conch shell, loud and clear, calling the people to church.

Lorenzo was one of the many people scattered through the jungle who survived by farming a tiny clearing and gathering such food as he could find that grew wild about him. He lived simply with a woman he had chosen years ago and their many children, some almost grown now. An untutored Spanish native working barefoot and tilling the soil, he knew nothing of God until one day when some members of the Pueblo Nuevo church, out on a walking expedition into the bush to do missionary work, came to his hut and began to tell him about Jesus. His soul cravings were stirred, and he became transformed almost at once. He began attending church every Sabbath, walking ten miles each way along the forest path.

He was like a man waiting for a train, and when that train came, he got on.

Ross gave him Bible studies, and when he explained the doctrine of baptism, Lorenzo begged to be baptized. "But there are a few things in your life that must be set right first," Ross told him.

"What are they? I want to belong to Jesus, and I will do anything!"

"You are not legally married," Ross explained. "You have been living with Emilita for years, but you have never been married."

"All right, so we will be married," he promised. True to his word, a few days later Lorenzo, Emilita, and all of the children walked the miles to Ancon, Canal Zone, where the couple could be married.

"Now," exclaimed Lorenzo, "we can be baptized!" Shortly thereafter he and his wife and the two oldest boys were baptized.

Lorenzo began going from one neighbor to another telling them about the gospel message, and soon he was meeting with a little group. Then he sent for the pastor to come to his village, a couple of miles beyond his home, where he had arranged to have a service held in the home of one of his friends.

When Ross got this appeal he was just recovering from malaria, the first of many such attacks, and he sent word he would come as soon as he was able to travel. After he had recovered sufficiently he walked out to the Pueblo Nuevo church on Friday and held the Sabbath services the next day. He spent the night in the minister's hut, and early Sunday morning he and a dozen or more church members started the twelve-mile hike to Lorenzo's village. Following a beaten path, they pushed steadily onward, walking single file, stopping only occasionally for a drink.

They reached Lorenzo's clearing about midmorning. In the center stood the hut, a thatched one-room affair made of palm trunks, bamboo, and other native material. Built up on stilts as a protection from wild animals, snakes, and insects, it was braced by long poles and stood on its frail legs in defiance of the wilderness around it. The family had been waiting for hours and now came out to greet the party, slowly, shyly, unaccustomed to visitors. Emilita brought out food, served with self-conscious eagerness, a meal for the hikers who were hungry and thirsty after the long, hot walk. Spread out before them like a picnic were foods from the garden and the jungle itself, and they ate heartily of boiled pigeon peas, baked yams, and corn grits cooked with coconut milk. For dessert they picked mangos from a tree at the edge of the clearing.

After eating, they began the walk to the village following a path that meandered past huts much like Lorenzo's, calling out as they passed each one, *"Síganos a la reunión* [Follow us to the meeting]." Many were willing to join the expedition and bobbed along the trail like a flock of brightly colored birds, chattering happily as they walked. As they came to each hut along the trail they called out the invitation, *"Síganos a la reunión,"* smiling and beckoning all the while. The more timid would skitter along at the end of the line, curious but a bit apprehensive about this new religion, while others slunk away to fade from sight in the trees when they saw the procession approaching.

"They are afraid the devils from us will get on them," Lorenzo explained.

Soon they arrived at the village, a nondescript collection of huts, one of which had been chosen for the service. It was simplicity itself, having no walls except on one side to block the wind from the cooking area. The bedroom was up on a rugged platform under the tangled, bug-infested roof where the family climbed up on notched poles to sleep.

The congregation sat on the floor. As Ross stood up before them he again felt the deep hunger these children of the jungle had for the Word of God. With a Spanish interpreter he preached on God's love using simple terms and illustrations they could understand. The response was overwhelming, and when he asked how many of them wanted to serve this loving God and change their heathen ways, they answered with an enthusiastic *"Sí, sí, señor!"* Many dedicated their lives to God's service, asking for a teacher to be sent to them, and several couples followed Lorenzo's example requesting marriage. This was the beginning of the work among the Spanish-speaking believers in that area.

Chapter 7
Panama City

Jacob next introduced Ross to the Panama City church, which was different from Colón in ethnic background. In Colón the majority was of West Indian descent and spoke English, while in Panama City fully half of the population were the Spanish-speaking nationals of the country. Because Jacob worked with the English-speaking people for the most part, he never learned Spanish, although at times street Spanish was almost a necessity for buying and traveling. However, he steadfastly refused to learn even that and sometimes ran into problems but usually managed to survive by his wits.

Jacob and Ross took the train from Colón to Panama City on the Sabbath morning of the first visit. As they were pulling into the station Jacob said, "We have to take a cab to the church. To let our Spanish cab driver know where we want to go, I have to tell him the name of the street. I never can pronounce it. Sounds to me like 'come in and go out.' "

The name of the street actually was Camino Ganou, which loosely means "cow path," but when the cab pulled up, the two men got in and Jacob slurred very rapidly, "Come in and go out." This was evidently close enough because they soon pulled up in front of the church.

A few weeks later when Ross came to this church to conduct the Sabbath service, he saw two of the ladies standing on opposite sides of the sanctuary glowering at each other. He had to pass each woman in turn as he walked down the aisle to reach the pastor's study. Elizabeth stood barring his way with clenched fists, her usually pleasant face drawn into a scowl. She glanced across at Martha and hissed in a stage whisper, "You see that woman over there? She struck me and cursed me."

Ross had only a few moments before Sabbath School would begin, so he said, "You come to my study after the service, and we will talk this over."

Then he walked by Martha, who also stopped him. Martha was very tall, angular, and somewhat stooped, and every Sabbath she wore a big white hat. The hat flopped now as she jerked her head and said hoarsely, "That woman over there is wicked. She hit me and threw rocks and even cursed." With folded arms and pursed lips she stood and regarded the pastor, who didn't have time right then to mediate the argument, so he told her also to come to his study right after church.

After the last hymn and the last Amen, Ross made his way to his study, where two sullen women were waiting for him. Elizabeth, short and round, was waiting on one side, and on the other was Martha, dark eyes smoldering in the thin face beneath the white hat. As Ross stood before them looking from one hostile face to the other, he knew the fine line an arbitrator must walk, for he must not only solve the problem, but he must at the last have the good will of all concerned. These women were mad. They were outraged. They were out for revenge. And they were both right. He laid his Bible on the desk, looked at his watch, and then at Martha and Elizabeth in turn. "Ladies," he began, "I have an appointment at another church shortly, but I am willing to cancel it in order to attend a funeral."

The eyes in the dark faces grew round with astonishment as they looked at him and then at each other with the unanswered question in the air. Who had died?

In solemn tones Ross continued, "We have come to this room to witness the death of two people."

Not a sound could be heard, and they sat there for several minutes in silence until Martha asked, "Elder, what . . . what do you mean?"

"I mean just what I said. When two women are dead we will leave this room." Again there was a long silence, and the tension between the women built.

Then Elizabeth looked up and began acidly, "I know I got angry and said some things I shouldn't have said, but—"

"There are no 'but's' in this death," Ross interrupted, sensing the blame shifting.

At this the two women looked at each other, and Elizabeth ran over to Martha, embracing her and sobbing, "It was all my fault. Please forgive me."

"No, it was my fault," insisted Martha. "I am so sorry for all the terrible things I said to you."

"Now they are dead," declared the pastor as they wept together. "Let us pray." Two penitent ladies knelt with their arms around one another while they asked God's forgiveness. Ross hurried on to Pueblo Nuevo for his next service.

One Sabbath Ross detained one of the deaconesses, Sister Walters, at the door. As he shook her hand he spoke seriously. "Maudy, we need help with the evangelistic meetings. Can we count on you?"

Startled by the request, she stammered, "Why, of course, Elder, but what can I do?"

"We are looking for Bible workers for this series of meetings we will be holding here in Panama City, and I thought of you right away." He had been impressed that she would be a great asset to this effort, for even though she had gone through persecution and disappointments, she remained a most godly person, having wonderful faith—direct, childlike, and unquestioning. Like many in that time and place, she lived always on the edge of poverty, but in spite of all her hardships, a radiant Christian character shone out of her that gave her great dignity.

Sister Walters was delighted. A smile lighted up her usually serious face, and she answered with enthusiasm, "Oh, Elder, I would love to." Then she dropped her eyes and a shadow crossed the strong, dark face. "But I haven't any shoes. My husband is not a believer, you know, and he won't give me any money to buy shoes because he thinks that will discourage me from coming to church. I can't represent the Lord without being properly dressed." She studied her bare toes sadly and, with a helpless little gesture, turned to go.

But Ross was not going to be put off by this, and with his usual zeal he exclaimed, "Wait, Maudy. I know the Lord wants you to help with these meetings. Come, let's go into my office and pray that He will send you some shoes. You believe He will, don't you?"

"Yes, sir, I do. He has answered my prayers so many times." So in the pastor's study they prayed for one pair of shoes.

A few days later Maudy was walking through the better part of the city, and as she passed the home of a well-to-do family where she used to work, she heard someone calling her name. Looking up, she saw Mrs. Richardson waving from the porch, a smile lighting up the kindly face. There was about her the air of one who has never had to think about money. "Maudy, Maudy," she called, "come in a minute. I'm so glad you came by. I bought a pair of shoes the other day, and they are too big for me. Would you care to try them on?" She held out the shoes, and Maudy was speechless as she touched them with one finger.

"Go ahead," Mrs. Richardson urged, "try them on." She handed the lovely brown shoes to Maudy. Hugging them to her, Maudy stared at them speechless. Sitting down at last, she tried them on, first one and then the other.

"I ordered them from England," Mrs. Richardson said. "Well, how do they fit?"

"Oh, they fit," Maudy exclaimed. "Of course, they fit. God wouldn't send me shoes that didn't fit."

Maudy told Ross about the answered prayer one day when he was making a pastoral visit, and after showing him the shoes, kept in the box and only to be worn to church, she said soberly, "Elder Sype, I wish you would talk to my Tim. He is getting so hard to manage. I can't even take him to church anymore because he is so naughty—always up to something."

Ross looked out the window and saw a little boy about six years old, scantily dressed, playing in a mud puddle. "Is that little Tim?" he asked.

"Yes, that's him. What can I do with him, Elder? You know my husband discourages him and me, too, from going to church in every way he can."

"Call him in," the young minister answered. "I'd like to talk with him."

Maudy went to the window and called. The little boy walked shyly into the room and stood by the door with his hands behind his back and his eyes cast down.

"Little Tim," Ross said kindly, "come here to me." The small boy sidled over to him and looked up with great, dark eyes, as the pastor put his arm around him.

"Timmy, do you love Jesus?" Ross asked.

Tim bashfully looked up and halfway nodded.

"Do you want to be a Jesus boy?" Again the nod of the curly little head.

"Will you come to Sabbath School next Sabbath?"

This time there was a mumbled, "Yes, sir."

"Fine. I'll be looking for you."

Tim ran out then to continue playing in his mud puddle, but the next Sabbath he was in church wearing a little white suit. He had a wide smile for the pastor, who put his arm on his shoulder and showed him to his class, saying as he left, "Now be good, Timmy, and I'll see you later."

When Ross shook Tim's hand after church he said, "I'll be looking for you next Sabbath." From that time on Little Tim never missed a Sabbath.

After Ross and Gertrude moved from Panama, they lost track of Little Tim. In 1954 at the General Conference session in San Francisco, Ross was walking down the corridor in the great convention hall and heard a voice behind him calling his name. Turning around, he saw a dark, well-dressed man who asked, "Aren't you Elder Sype who used to be in Panama?"

Wondering who this tall, dignified stranger could be, Ross replied, "Yes, I am."

"I am Little Tim," replied the man with a chuckle, for at six feet two he towered over his old pastor and was now Elder Walters in the ministry in Costa Rica.

That was not the last time he saw Little Tim, for while visiting Jamaica in 1972 Ross again met Elder Walters, then president of the West Indian Union Conference. "Elder Walters," he exclaimed, "how wonderful to meet you again!"

"Don't call me Elder Walters. Call me Little Tim. You know, Elder Sype, if it hadn't been for you and my mother's prayers, I might still be in that mud puddle." The rich laughter rang out as he clasped Ross's hand. "Yes, sir, you must always call me Little Tim."

Chapter 8
Gertrude and Marie

Ross was buoyed up by the challenges of missionary life in a new and different place. Hiking down jungle paths to bring the message of God's love to remote villages, he was living out a dream. Gertrude had come fully intending to like this new place, but as one hot soggy day followed another, she found her spirits flagging. The only bright spot was Marie, who had recently come to Panama with her husband, J. P. Greene, the new publishing secretary. He had come to take the place of Jacob Osborne, who had gone back to the United States. A friendship blossomed between the two women. It was one of those unique friendships that often develop when two people of similar background meet in some far-flung place and find they are on the same wavelength.

"I never thought missionary life was going to be this—well—boring," Gertrude said to Marie one long, hot afternoon.

Marie nodded and sighed, smoothed a pillow on the couch, and looked out the window. "Before we came I thought we would have work to do, excitement at every turn, but our husbands have all the excitement. Nobody told us what it was like for the wives."

"At home we had our familiar church, jobs, family, things to do. We could go shopping. But here . . .

"Another thing. I'm sick and tired of what the brochures call 'lush, tropical foliage.' " Gertrude glared out the window at the palm trees as if they were responsible. "And the same climate day after day after day. What wouldn't I give for a cold November day in Iowa with the wind blowing and the clouds scudding across a gray sky."

50

Marie followed her gaze out the window. "I never liked November—until now, but I miss weather changes too. I mean, big weather changes. Not from hot to hotter but from hot to cold. Putting your summer clothes away, getting out your winter things. And the food—I dream of chocolate ice cream. Remember that chocolate ice cream we used to get at that little place in Nevada at camp meeting time?"

Gertrude gave a little moan. "One morning I woke up thinking I could smell the hot buns my mother made for breakfast. She made them for me that last morning I was home. And what wouldn't I give for a piece of apple pie. I suppose for Thanksgiving we could make pumpkin pie out of yams, but I haven't seen an apple since I got here."

"This may sound silly, but I miss American slang, and those little dress shops. Walking up and down between the aisles looking at the latest fashions. If I had only brought a Sears catalog." Marie yawned broadly and blurted out, "I was braced for adversity, even trouble—but not inertia."

"You know, I always thought Nevada, Iowa, was sort of a dull little place, but I was busy there. And I had my sisters."

"At least we have each other, Gertrude."

"That's one blessing. I am thankful for that. If we could only stir something up. "

"This may sound funny coming from me, but right now I would consider a Dorcas meeting in the church basement making quilts high drama."

"That's pretty pathetic for someone who doesn't even sew."

The mood persisted even the next morning when they met at the market. "The market always reminds me of my brother, Merle," Gertrude said. "He's a gardener. Sells produce door to door—tomatoes, green onions, cucumbers—nothing like this, of course. Says he's going to have his own fruit stand someday. Maybe even a store. He'd love this place." She picked up a mango and turned it around in her hands. "I'd trade everything here for a plain old Iowa radish."

Carrying their bags of produce, they walked slowly home. When they passed the local movie theater, Marie clutched Gertrude's arm and said, "Look, Gertrude, an American movie. *The Birth of a Nation* with Lillian Gish. I read about it before we came. Everybody in the States was talking about it." She looked at the sign, turned pleading eyes to Gertrude, and looked back at the sign.

"Oh no, Marie," Gertrude said. "Forget that. You know what Ross and J. P. think about movies."

"Oh, sure. They're out there doing important things while we . . . oh, Gertrude," and she lapsed into a whine. "Something from home would do us a world of good. I'm so homesick I could cry."

"Well, I guess it would cheer us up," Gertrude said slowly. "And you know what the Bible says, 'a merry heart doeth good like a medicine.' " They exchanged a conspiratorial look, and then in her impulsive way she added, "Come on, Marie. Let's not dawdle. We have to make plans before the boys come home."

Energized by the idea of the movie, they forgot the heat. "We'll have to go in disguise, of course, and Marie, no matter what, even on your deathbed, you are not to tell J. P., ever."

Marie turned wide, innocent eyes on her friend. "Oh, I wouldn't think of it."

"I hope not. Still, I don't know about you. Anyway, nothing is going to stop us now. How can we look like Panamanians?"

"Easy. I can borrow a dress from my maid. She's tall for a native from here. But finding one in your size might be tricky," Marie said. "You're so, well, you know, you tower over the men in the streets here. Now, don't be offended. In America an attractive, statuesque woman like you looks like a fashion model, but here . . ."

Gertrude was well aware she didn't fit the petite, feminine ideal of the compliant woman. She was a strong woman, a bit intimidating, but she had grown up in a big family where you had to hold your own. She shrugged and gave an airy wave. "Anyway, I do have a dress. I bought one at the market to take home and show my sisters. Nobody in our family is tiny, so I got the biggest one they had. I'm all set. A head scarf, dark glasses, and off we go."

Marie giggled excitedly. "I'll wear that red wig I found up in the closet. Left by some other missionary wife, I suppose. I came close to throwing it out, but for some reason didn't. For this, I guess."

They decided to go the next Wednesday afternoon when the men would be out in the field until late. Dressing at Gertrude's house, they put on their disguises and walked around the room before the mirror, turning this way and that. "Our own mothers wouldn't know us," Gertrude assured her conspirator. Brimming with eagerness, they stepped out the door and headed down the street, confident they looked like two local women on their way to market. If heads turned to watch them go by, they took no notice.

They reached the theater, and with her hand on the door, Marie gave a little gasp and spun around. "Gertrude, keep going. Look who's coming," she whispered wildly. Gertrude froze as she saw the head deaconess of the church, Sister Plata, headed right for them, walking a little faster than usual.

"Merciful heavens," she muttered, remembering very well her first encounter with that good sister. She was their first caller when they moved into their house in Colón, and she had found Gertrude home alone unpacking as Ross had gone to the post office. Sister Plata had come to welcome them, ostensibly bringing fruit, but in reality to fill Gertrude in on the shortcomings of previous pastors' wives, which seemed to have been many. When Ross came home and saw the fruit, he asked where she had gotten it. "We had a visitor," she said. "Now I know what they mean by Greeks bearing gifts."

Here the sister was now, a conspirator's worst nightmare, headed right for them. "Don't look up," Gertrude hissed. "She'll never recognize us." Turning the other way they pretended to be interested in something down the street.

Mrs. Plata, however, stepped around in front of them, smiled in a calculating way, and with a stiff, formal bow said, "Good afternoon Mrs. Sype. Good afternoon, Mrs. Greene."

Too stunned to croak out a reply, they watched her depart. "How did she know it was us?" Marie asked.

"Marie, look at me. I mean, really, look at me. Do I look like I'm from here?"

"Frankly, no, and I'm sure I don't either. Do you suppose everybody in this town saw through our disguise?"

"Apparently everybody but us, carried away as we were. Oh, Marie, you should see yourself in that wig. You look like you escaped from the circus."

"And you—those big, pink feet bulging out from those sandals—and really there's nobody built like you in this whole town."

"We thought we were tripping along like those dainty little native donkeys when in reality we were lumbering like a couple of Iowa draft horses."

They began laughing then, doubling over, leaning against the building. "We better get for home before we meet someone else or get arrested," Gertrude gasped.

Once home, Marie said, "Well, we had our fun and didn't put our reputations on the line to boot."

Gertrude pulled her tight sandals off and rubbed her feet. "You know, Sister Plata might have been an angel sent to keep us from committing greater folly."

"What if she had been a second later and caught us buying our tickets?"

"It would have been all over the Isthmus by nightfall, you can be sure of that. We can thank the good Lord who looks after fools and adventurers."

Marie peeled the red wig from her head and, rubbing her scalp, said, "That probably won't be our last lark, but next time let's try to find something we can tell Ross and J. P. about."

Chapter 9
"Don't Send for Us If You Get in Trouble"

One morning as she sat at breakfast, Marie was startled by a loud pounding at the door. Peeking out, she saw a distraught Gertrude on her doorstep. "Gertrude?" she said, opening the door to let her in. "What on earth is wrong?"

"You won't believe this!" Gertrude said, bursting into the room.

"Believe what?" Marie asked, still half asleep.

"What would Jasper Wayne say to this?" Gertrude stormed, striding across the room while the bewildered Marie pushed her tangled dark hair back from her face.

"Jasper Wayne," repeated Marie vacantly. "I don't think I have had the pleasure—"

"Oh, now surely you know who Jasper Wayne is. *The* Jasper Wayne, the man who started the Harvest Ingathering program."

"Of course, the man from your home state. Sit down and tell me why you are so excited. Is he here?" Marie looked around as if she expected him to walk in the door.

"Actually, what I am trying to say has nothing to do with Jasper Wayne." Gertrude sat down and began fanning herself.

"You could have fooled me," Marie said, her interest beginning to pick up. She poured two glasses of orange juice. "Here, drink this and then let's go back to the beginning." They sat at the kitchen table as they had so many times since Marie had come to Panama.

"What I am really upset about is Ingathering," Gertrude began, trying to speak slowly. "I thought we could start now that fall is here—you know how tired we are of staying home all of the time doing nothing. But now I find out that the conference has never had an Ingathering program and, in fact, doesn't think the people here would approve of it."

"What!" exclaimed Marie. "They won't let you go ingathering? I never heard of such a thing." Although she had never been too enthusiastic about going out back home, now that it was forbidden, Marie found her interest was piqued.

"To think of the people I've reached and the dollars and dollars I've solicited over the years," Gertrude continued. "Back in Iowa, Ross's mother and I went out every fall. I just knew that was one way I could be of help here, and then to find out they are afraid it will offend the people."

"Offend the people, indeed!" exclaimed Marie. "Who do they think they are? Our workers all over the world are engaging in ingathering while here . . ." She sputtered to a stop and then went on. "Just wait until I tell J. P., if he ever comes back from his trip, that is."

Now that she had the backing and support of her friend, there was no stopping Gertrude, and she turned to Marie with flashing eyes. "Let's show those men in the conference it can be done! We'll go to Panama City and solicit the business district!"

"Oh, do you think we should go that far?"

"Why not? Think how surprised they'll be when we come back with our purses full of money! It isn't just about money, either. The money is secondary. This is missionary work. Getting out among the people and telling them about our work. Asking them to church."

"One person to another. That's what it's all about, isn't it? Jesus called the disciples. They called someone else. Someone called me, and I must call someone."

"Exactly. We may just be the wives, but don't forget, we are missionary wives."

Hesitant at first, Marie warmed to the plan as Gertrude talked, and at last she said, "All right. I'll help you. I want to keep busy while J. P. is away so I won't get lonesome. Besides, it is a good cause."

Ross tried to persuade them to abandon what seemed to him a fool-hardy scheme, but when he found they were determined to go ahead, he insisted they go through the proper channels and take the matter before the conference brethren. Some people thought that women were becoming a little troublesome in the early 1920s. In America they had gotten the right to vote, and here were two ambitious ladies trying to go ahead of the policies prescribed by men for the church. Gertrude and Marie outlined their proposal to the committee and, between them, barnstormed their way through all objections. Permission was at last grudgingly given and a promise that two passes for Panama City would be at the depot in time for departure in the morning. Two elated women walked out smiling their thanks, while a roomful of men sat in frustrated silence.

Gertrude and Marie came to the station the next morning bubbling over with good spirits. When they arrived at the station they received a devastating blow. The passes were not there. Instead, they found a curt note informing them that after thinking it over the committee had rescinded their decision, and the passes were not going to be issued. They stood inside the dingy little depot, too stunned to speak. They looked bleakly at each other and up and down the track, past frail little houses leaning together on long legs like tired herons. Far in the distance they heard a train whistle. Gertrude sat down heavily and exclaimed, "Can you beat that!"

"And after they had promised," Marie wailed. The train whistled again, closer now. Gertrude leaped to her feet and declared in a tone that would muster the troops, "They can't do this to us! Marie, are you game to go on our own?"

Marie stared in amazement at her friend and then said, "Yes, of course, but where will we get the money? I haven't a cent." She spread her hands helplessly.

"I haven't either," Gertrude replied stoutly, "but they are not going to stop us now. Look, I have a plan. I know a lady who lives in an apartment near here. I'll run up and ask her if she'll loan us ten dollars until we get back from Panama City this afternoon. You stay here. I'll be right back," she called over her shoulder.

"Hurry!" Marie shrieked. "I hear the train whistle getting closer."

The steam engine came puffing into the station, ground to a stop, and idled with dramatic impatience while people got off and the baggage was unloaded. Just when the passengers were getting on, a breathless Gertrude came running up, triumphantly waving a ten-dollar bill.

The first day of ingathering in Panama City was successful far beyond their expectations. Ignoring the heat, the flies, and the rude stares that sometimes followed them, they went from one business to another. Instead of encountering the promised resistance and hostility, they were greeted by smiling shopkeepers, who took the leaflets they handed out with a *"Gracias, señora,"* and gave liberally to the cause. Their purses were filling up with money. Arriving back home later in the day, they emptied them on the table and jubilantly counted out $114.53. When Marie and Gertrude made their report to the conference officials, those gentlemen were amazed at the success of this venture. Realizing the potential of the program, they promptly named Gertrude home missionary secretary.

Gertrude plunged into her new duties and sent letters to all of the churches urging them to take part in Ingathering. Marie, too, bubbled over with new life at this activity. As they went over the plans one day Gertrude had a new inspiration. "Marie, let's take an ingathering trip to Bocas del Toro and Costa Rica. No one has ever worked in those places. There must be people there who are looking for something beyond this life. People who would like to help our mission."

"Sounds like a great idea, but what about our husbands? Will they think so, or will they think it's just another of our mad schemes?"

"I'm sure we can sweet-talk them into it."

"But I've never asked to go on such a long trip without J. P. before, and out of the country at that. He'll think I have lost my senses," Marie ended lamely, beginning to flag at this daring enterprise.

Gertrude's enthusiasm never dulled. "You're a grown woman, Marie, not a child who has to ask permission for everything. He should be proud of the part you're playing in this new program. We are pioneers. We can't give up now."

Gertrude's optimism was short-lived, for when she outlined the plan to Ross he emphatically condemned the whole idea. Having just returned from an itinerary in that area, he was well aware of the problems they might encounter.

"You don't know what you're talking about. You have never been in that country," he said, pacing around the room. "You have no idea of the dangers involved. You will be leaving yourselves wide open to any number of hazardous situations—assault, robbery, even malaria—just to name a few."

He turned toward her and began to speak more slowly, "I cannot understand how two sensible and, I thought, intelligent women could throw caution to the wind and come up with such a harebrained idea!"

"It is not a harebrained idea. What is wrong with Marie and me going on a trip to ingather? We were certainly able to take care of ourselves when we went to Panama City, and we can take care of ourselves in Bocas del Toro and Costa Rica. The Lord can protect us as He has you. Besides, those people need the message, our work needs the funds, and someone has to go out and make the contacts."

"What if you can't get a boat when you need one? Steamships are not traveling since the war, and native boats are never on schedule," Ross reminded her.

To which Gertrude replied with the magnificent confidence of the young and inexperienced, "We'll just get a hotel room and wait until a boat shows up."

Meanwhile Marie was having an even harder time convincing her husband. But she persisted until he finally said, "All right. I'll tell you what I'll do. We'll go over to the Sypes', and if Ross has agreed to this crazy idea, I'll give you my blessing."

After a lively session in which the women refuted every argument presented by their husbands, Ross and J. P. conceded defeat. "But don't send for us if you get in trouble," were their last words on the subject.

That afternoon Gertrude and Marie hurried triumphantly down to the wharf and found a boat leaving for Costa Rica. They booked passage and at the appointed time were on board. After docking at Limón, they had supper in a Spanish restaurant that delighted the romantic Marie, and then they found a comfortable hotel.

"Imagine the fellows putting up such a fuss. Everything is going great," Gertrude sighed contentedly as she put the light out.

"They just don't want to admit we can get along without them," Marie said, yawning. "Oh, I am so tired after all of that fussing around this morning and then the boat ride. But it has been fun so far."

The next morning they were out working the business district early. The town was beautiful, the people friendly, and they were having incredible success in telling about the work and getting contributions. Before returning to their hotel room that afternoon they made arrangements for passage to Bocas del Toro. They arrived in that city early the next morning and began ingathering in the business district. The men responded with money and smiles and seemed eager to read the tracts they handed out.

As the heat of the afternoon bore down, the shops began closing, so they decided to go and find passage back to Colón. Gertrude, buoyed up by the sweet taste of success, said eagerly, "Maybe we can get a boat leaving this afternoon. I can hardly wait to get home and see what Ross and J. P. have to say about the great ingatherers."

Marie giggled and replied, "I just can't get over the way those men made such a fuss—all that talk about . . . what was it Ross said? Assault, robbery, malaria? Talk about calamity howlers! It has been lovely here. Just like going on vacation." She gave a little skip as they walked along.

"Really, you would think they were jealous. It isn't like it used to be, you know. Women are starting to stand up and be counted," Gertrude smiled smugly as she spoke.

"We have certainly proved ourselves on this trip," said Marie, giving her heavy purse a little shake as they turned toward the docks to find a boat to Colón.

Not thinking anything could go wrong, they made their way, laughing and talking, down the path that led to the harbor, a sorry-looking place surrounded by shacks thrown together from any available material. The town was set on a key and sprawled out on all sides, low to the water and mosquito ridden. Nearing the docks, they became aware of the unsavory atmosphere of the place and were soon talking in whispers and looking nervously from side to side as they stepped around men lying in the pathway, sleeping or drunk. "Snaky looking place, isn't it?" Marie whispered, drawing closer to Gertrude.

Just then Gertrude spotted a small building with a sign in Spanish above the door. "I think this is the place we can see about our boat to Colón," she said as they stepped inside. A man was sitting at a desk shuffling through some papers. He looked up when the women entered and smiled broadly as he greeted the Americans, but after some struggle with his English and their Spanish, one thing was certain—there was no boat to Colón that afternoon nor any afternoon in the near future. Gertrude and Marie looked at each other in dismay, and the man said he was sorry and spread his hands and shrugged his shoulders, but what could he do?

Back out on the street in the fading light of day, the sobering truth came to them. They were alone in Bocas del Toro, where crime and poverty were a way of life—two defenseless women with a lot of money. They became aware of men watching their progress through heavy lidded eyes with more than casual interest. As they made their way from the shabby docks, where the spars of boats stood in the bay like skeletons and gulls screamed, they felt very small and vulnerable. The final words of Ross and J. P. rang in their ears, "Don't send for us if you get in trouble."

They turned slowly and walked away, becoming increasingly aware of the decadence around them, noticing about the town a certain disquieting sleaziness they hadn't seen in the morning when they had rushed from store to store. Enterprising and capable businessmen carried on a thriving trade in the city during the day, but now, as night was falling, the frightened ingatherers saw dark and ragged men who roamed the streets at night looking for food, and the hard faces of women, looking old and toothless at forty, who stared at these strangers as they picked their way along the littered streets. Men who lived by stealth watched their progress. Evil hung in the air.

"It seems I've heard Ross say something about a train somewhere in this vicinity. Maybe we can take it to a port where we can get a boat," Gertrude suggested hopefully as they walked along. But this idea led to another dead end, for they found the nearest locomotive was a narrow-gauge train across the lagoon at Almirante that went to the banana plantations at Guabito, the opposite of the way they wanted to go.

"What are we going to do now?" Marie asked in desperation.

"We'll have to get a hotel room. We don't want to be out on these streets after dark."

"We don't even want to be out here in broad daylight!" Marie was beginning to sniffle and dab at her eyes.

"Stop whimpering," Gertrude retorted sharply. "I'm sorry, Marie, but you can't let people like this know you are afraid. Stop rolling your eyes. Talk. Smile." She led the way, walking briskly. "Let's go back to that hotel we solicited earlier and get a room."

"Oh, why didn't I listen to J. P.?" Marie moaned as they walked into the lobby of the dirty little hotel, where faded, dusty chairs were grouped before the fly-specked windows. Two men slouched on a couch over in a corner exchanging meaningful looks as the two women entered. The tall one stood up to greet them in Spanish, bowing in an insolent manner, while both men fastened ferret eyes on the full purses. Thoroughly frightened now, Gertrude and Marie were escorted to their room by a dark, surly native wearing ragged clothes. His bold eyes took note of their clothes, good shoes, and fat handbags as he handed them the key. Upon entering the room they slammed the flimsy door shut, and Marie slipped the makeshift bolt in place. Her face was pale and her hands trembled. "Gertrude, did you see those men in the lobby?" she wailed.

"Yes, they think we are rich Americans," whispered Gertrude.

"Why did we wear our good clothes?" Marie cried, pushing back her hair with unsteady hands.

"What would it matter? They think all Americans are rich," Gertrude replied with a shake of her head. "Besides those men in the lobby, we have the hotel clerk to think about too. I wouldn't want to meet him in a dark alley." She shivered slightly, remembering how the wanton eyes had appraised them.

She sprang to her feet suddenly, exclaiming, "Come on, Marie. Help me move this dresser against the door." She began tugging frantically at the ancient piece of furniture built of heavy wood. Together they pushed and tugged until they had it against the door. The dark tropical night came down, and they said their prayers, asking the Lord's protection. Finally they dozed into a restless sleep.

They spent a long, uneasy night in the rather broken-down bed they had to share in the shabby room. There were strange rustling sounds between roof and ceiling, voices in the street of late-returning drunks, a woman's scream. Dogs barked, and once footsteps in the hall just outside their room woke Marie, who sat up and clutched Gertrude's arm. "What's that?" she rasped. She got up to look for a weapon and, seeing nothing better, brought their shoes to bed. "It's not much, but at least we can clobber them with these if we have to."

Awakening at daybreak, stiff and tired, they dressed quickly. For worship, Gertrude turned to Psalm 91 and began to read: " 'Surely he shall deliver thee from the snare of the fowler, and from the noisome pestilence. He shall cover thee with his feathers, and under his wings shalt thou trust: . . . Thou shalt not be afraid of the terror by night; nor for the arrow that flieth by day; . . . There shall no evil befall thee . . . For he shall give his angels charge over thee' " (verses 3–11). The psalm had never meant more to either of them. After kneeling for prayer, they stood up, and Gertrude said, "Chin up, Marie, God is looking after us."

"Has to be God. I really didn't have too much faith in those shoes last night."

"Now we must have faith that He will get us out of this dreadful place," Gertrude said soberly as she picked up her things, preparing to leave. Marie, already packed, was sitting in one of the rickety chairs, writing furiously. "Whatever are you doing?" Gertrude cried. "Let's get out of here!"

Marie looked up from her scribbling and sniffed, and when she spoke, her voice quivered. "I'm writing to J. P. and telling him if I ever get back to Colón alive, I'll never do anything against his wishes again."

At that Gertrude snorted. "You can write that if you want to, but I'd never put something like that on paper to Ross. I'd never hear the end of it. Come on, help me push this dresser away from the door."

They walked from their room, through the lobby, and out onto the streets of the shabby little town. Not knowing where else to turn, they decided to go to the American consul for help. After some inquiry they found the office and the consul himself, a round little man absorbed in a book and a dish of peppermints. As they poured out their story, his face took on new life. Making sympathetic clicking sounds, he pushed the dish of peppermints toward them. His stagnating job here was insufferably dull. He waited day after day for some other appointment to come through, so he was overjoyed at any diversion. He leaped to the task of rescuing two lovely ladies in distress and managed to book passage for them on a small boat going to Colón. Then he gallantly escorted them down to the dock and bade them farewell. As the little craft pulled away from the wharf, the good consul waved his wide straw hat as if bidding goodbye to old friends.

The boat plowed through the seas. Gertrude and Marie sat on the deck relaxing in the late afternoon sunshine while fresh breezes blew over them. For the first time in what seemed like many days, they felt safe and at peace.

In good spirits now that they were on their way home, they talked about their homecoming and the adventures of the last few days while they watched the crew going about their tasks with the smooth, easy grace of men working at a job they know.

"Isn't the captain handsome?" Marie said after he walked by and bowed stiffly. He was a slim, proud figure in a uniform so white it sparkled against the blue sky and the sea.

"Oh, yes," Gertrude agreed, "a real Spanish *caballero.*"

After a while Gertrude grew strangely silent and sat with her eyes fixed on the distant horizon while Marie rambled on. "It was so good of the consul to find us this lovely boat. Oh, look at the sunset. The sun is dropping right into the sea like a ball of fire. I always imagine I can hear it sizzle," she said with a giggle, and turned to find Gertrude looking miserable and pale and wiping sweat from her forehead. The small boat was pitching in the long swells of the Caribbean, and Gertrude, who was prone to seasickness, began to feel a familiar queasiness. Marie was alarmed and asked anxiously, "Whatever is the matter? You look positively green."

Gertrude lurched to her feet and staggered to the rail with her hand clasped over her mouth, all the while making horrible gurgling sounds, and then with a force that began at her toes, she threw up all she had eaten that day. She did not see the ship's officer, the proud, handsome *caballero,* standing there deep in contemplation, his snowy white, immaculate uniform outlined against the sky. She aimed at the sea, but with a little lurch of the ship, it was the captain who got the full brunt of her day's repast. He gasped and stepped back, and then, showing noble self-control, he gallantly escorted the stricken passenger back to her deck chair. Although his uniform was dripping, he bowed low and refused to listen to her apologies. "Forget it, *señora.* It is nothing. I know it is bad to be sick." He pronounced it "seek" and smiled reassuringly, bowed again, and with great dignity walked away.

Marie's blue eyes had been growing rounder and rounder, and as the stiff back disappeared toward the officer's quarters, she doubled up and screamed with laughter. Gertrude sat in limp and utter dejection while waves of embarrassment rolled over her. Glancing at Marie with disgust she muttered, "Fine friend you turned out to be."

"I'm sorry, but you should have seen the look on his face," she shrilled, making an unsuccessful effort to control her mirth.

"Oh, if I ever meet him face to face, I will just die!" Gertrude groaned, her head in her hands.

Before they dropped off to sleep that night Gertrude said, "Marie, if you ever mention this to anyone, I'll . . . I'll . . ." Marie was quick to assure her she would never tell a soul, a promise she promptly forgot once they were safely back in port.

The next morning they were up to see the sun rise out of the sea, and they thought of the safe haven of home and the reunion with their husbands. Marie opened the porthole to let the fresh sea breeze in to sweeten the warm air of the tiny cabin. Overjoyed now that the adventure was safely over, she flung out her arms as she exclaimed, "Ah, the salt spray of the sea, fresh air—gorgeous day, isn't it? And all our tomorrows will be as bright."

"You are the poetic one this morning, but I hope you're right," was Gertrude's terse reply, her gaze fixed on an outline of green growing larger against the sky. "Don't forget, in just a few hours we will have to do a lot of explaining to Ross and J. P. I can see it now. Every time we get one of our brilliant ideas, they will say, 'Now, my dear, remember Bocas del Toro.' "

Chapter 10
The Brave Gringo

Gertrude's work as home missionary secretary ground to a halt after the adventure in Bocas, and she was forced to carry on her work by correspondence, but that was not her way. She chaffed under restraint. She wanted to be on the firing line. As soon as she got a message from Ross, she rushed over to Marie's apartment. Bursting in, she exclaimed, "Oh, Marie, what a stroke of luck. Now we can get back to work and get on with our ingathering."

Marie looked at her with interest, for she was beginning to languish in the long, hot, idle days. "Well, anything for some excitement. Come on, sit down and tell me what you are cooking up now."

"I can hardly believe this myself, but I just got a message from Ross. He is holding meetings in Bocas and said we could come and finish the ingathering."

She paused, waiting for Marie's approval, but what she got was a look of horror. Marie pushed her chair back as if to escape, saying in a strangled voice, "What, go back to Bocas? Are you crazy? I wouldn't go back there for a million dollars!"

"Now, Marie," Gertrude began soothingly, "it will be entirely different this time. For one thing, Ross will be there to help us." She reached for an orange and began to peel it with a small knife.

Marie watched the orange peel form into a long curl while her memories of that terrifying night in Bocas went through her mind. "But Bocas . . ." she began and gave a little shiver. "It was so awful—those people—I just don't want to go there again ever."

"Ross is going to be working in the outlying areas," Gertrude explained, "and we will work in the town itself and finish up what we started there. We did get a good response from the businessmen. Remember how eager they were to read the literature about our work?"

A spark of interest showed in Marie's face, and then she stiffened and shook her head and wailed dismally, "But where would we stay? In that miserable little hotel with that horrible clerk creeping about and those criminals down in the lobby just waiting for nightfall? Nothing doing!"

"Now wait," Gertrude said. "I haven't told you the best part yet. Ross has fixed up the old mission house for us to stay in. He says it is lovely and in a good part of town. Please say you will go. I really need you, and besides ingathering at Bocas, we will get to go up to Almirante and Guabito. It will be like a vacation."

"Well," Marie began slowly, "it does sound like fun, and I am getting bored silly and lonesome, too, with J. P. gone to the interior. All right, I may live to regret it, but I'll go."

"Good! Great! Start packing. The boat leaves this afternoon, and we will be gone for ten days or so."

At the prospect of a trip Marie began to cheer up. She shouted as Gertrude hurried away, "Now you can tell Ross your good news in person."

Ross met them at the dock and took them to the mission house. It was surprisingly cozy and comfortable. Ross's term "lovely" was stretching the description a bit, but the house was certainly a step up from the hotel.

Although Gertrude was going to wait for the perfect time to tell her husband some news, she could hold out no longer. When he was showing her their room she began, "I am really glad to be here so I can tell you the great news. I have been knitting little things."

"Knitting," he repeated blankly. "I didn't know you knew how to knit."

"Knitting *little* things," she repeated slowly. "Don't you get it?"

He stared at her as if she had lost her mind, and she laughed and said, "For the baby—for our baby."

"What . . . what . . . are you sure—you mean—?"

"That's right. I went to the doctor in Colón this week, and he was positive. We are going to have a baby."

Ross was stunned and could only say, "After seven years of marriage. I can hardly believe it."

"The natives say it's the climate!"

All went well with ingathering this time at Bocas. The ladies were blessed there as well as at Almirante and Guabito. Ross's series of meetings were drawing to a close, and on that last night Marie stayed at the mission house to rest. Ross and Gertrude walked the short distance to the meeting.

The meeting that night began like any other. After a rousing song service Ross stood up before the congregation and was just warming to his subject, when a sudden loud crash brought the sermon to an abrupt halt. The minister lifted questioning eyes, and the church members froze in their seats as rocks bombarded the building.

To understand why Ross's meetings might run into antagonism, it is necessary to know something about the racial and religious factions of Bocas del Toro at that time. The English-speaking West Indian inhabitants outnumbered the Spanish speakers, who were mostly of the peasant type. This Spanish element, Catholic for the most part, was hostile not only toward the Protestant religions but also toward Americans. Although a few of the officials were white, the town leaders were largely of mixed blood, partly Caucasian, partly Indian, and partly African black. The membership of the Seventh-day Adventist church, set off to one side of the city, was made up almost entirely of West Indian people. The meetings had gone along smoothly with little trouble, probably due to the solicitations of Marie and Gertrude and also the visiting that Ross had done earlier. However, at the final service a hard-core Spanish group decided to make an attack.

The first assault was followed by a second and then a third. Several well-aimed rocks came crashing through a window, sending shards of glass splintering through the air. Men shouted outside, the voices muffled at first and then louder.

"*¡Saquémosle el corazón! ¡Saquémosle!*" ("Cut the gringo's heart out! Cut it out!") a man's voice yelled out, loud above the other voices.

The mob took up a chant. "*¡Abajo con el gringo! ¡Abajo con el gringo!*" ("Down with the *gringo!* Down with the *gringo!*" With a fury that knew no reason, they surrounded the little church in Bocas del Toro.

Ross walked down the aisle from the platform and moved resolutely toward the door. Gertrude watched him with mounting dread and, catching hold of him as he passed, said in terror, "You can't go out there. Please don't go. They will kill you!"

"I have to," he answered, breaking away from her. "I have no choice. If they think we're afraid, we'll never be able to work here again. If I confront them, I will hopefully gain their respect. This is just a devilish scheme to force us out."

The members begged him not to go. "Elder, they will kill you. They are very wicked. Don't go out," they entreated.

But he went. Pausing at the door, he looked back at the congregation and said, "Pray for me." Then he walked out and faced the mob. Standing on the steps of the church, he looked into their faces. The leader was a known trouble-maker named Manuel, a small man who made quick, nervous movements. With his big ears, shifty little eyes, and malevolent grin, he looked rather like a runt pig. Close beside him stood Juan, second in command of this rag-tag bunch of ruffians. Long hair curled around a darkly handsome face in a care-less, battle-scarred way, his nose a little off center, broken at some time in a brawl. He was armed with sticks and stones and a big mouth.

"Down with the *gringo*," shouted the leader.

"Down with the *gringo*," chorused the mob. The tumult grew to a deafen-ing pitch.

Ross put his hand in his hip pocket and began to speak, "Now, fellows, we are holding a meeting here and need to have it quiet. If you don't want to come in and listen, you must go by the time I count to three. *Uno, dos, tres.*" Assuming he had a gun in his pocket, the mob fled in a panic. In their haste to get away they ran into one another, some tripping and falling, and crawled and clawed their way out and at last disappeared. The night swallowed them up, quiet returned to the church, and Ross walked back inside and finished his sermon with no more interruptions.

While walking back to the mission house after the meeting, Ross said, "Too bad Marie didn't come with us tonight. She always likes a little excitement."

"It is probably just as well. I had to do a lot of talking to get her back here at all, even with the protection of the 'brave *gringo*.'"

He laughed and patted his hip pocket, reminding her, "You mean the brave, *armed gringo*." Then assuming a serious tone he repeated softly, " 'He shall call upon me, and I will answer him: I will be with him in trouble; I will deliver him' " (Psalm 91:15).

Chapter 11
The Bethel Church

With only primitive communications available in Panama, it never ceased to amaze Ross how the gospel message had been planted and taken root in some of the most remote, unheard-of places. There was no telephone, airplane, radio, or regular postal service. His next mission trip was to a place he had never heard of and couldn't find on a map. When he received a letter telling him to go to Bethel to hold services, he had to ask around to find out where it was and how to get there.

Ross had orders to wait on the dock at Bocas del Toro for a boat to pick him up. Standing in the shade of a ramshackle building, he watched boats sailing to and fro while men shouted and gulls screamed and dived. He liked everything about boat travel, even waiting on the dock, but he did want to get under way and relax on deck while the boat skimmed over the waters. Beginning to get apprehensive as boats came and went, Ross despaired of getting to Bethel that day. When he saw a tiny canoe bouncing over the waves of the Chiriqui Lagoon manned by two natives, he watched with detached interest. As the canoe approached the men pointed at him, said something to each other, and waved, and he realized with some dismay that this craft would take him to the Bethel church, some fourteen miles out over the waters.

They drew up to the dock, and one of the paddlers called out, "Are you Elder Sype?" Ross nodded and eyed the frail little dugout canoe that danced lightly on the waves.

"We take you to Bethel for afternoon service," the tall, thin man in the bow called out. He crawled out and held the canoe against the pilings, looking expectantly at Ross.

The man in the stern, who was younger and had a bright, eager smile, held up four fingers and said, "Meeting at four o'clock. We better go now."

Holding on to the dock, Ross let himself down gingerly into the tiny craft that was close to the water and moving playfully beneath him. Once on board, he held on to the gunnels with both hands as the homemade canoe skipped across the lake, spraying water on him each time it hit a wave.

Of all the churches to which Gertrude had sent Ingathering letters the previous year, none had responded more enthusiastically than the Bethel church. Ross had been anxious to visit this body of believers and see what motivated them so, and now he was about to find out.

The men were experts with the paddle as they were born to it, and they shot through the water. But still it was a long, tiring voyage. They swept by wild-looking keys, low to the water, where thin, stooped men and women tended small patches of corn, yams, and pigeon peas. Naked children played under the trees or in the water along the shore. Similar canoes came and went, manned by men and boys sitting with careless nonchalance, loaded with coconuts. Ross felt he would never know the same feeling of calm as he clasped the gunnels to keep his balance. After they had been paddling for some time he asked how much farther it was to Bethel.

The man in the bow pointed ahead and replied, "See that building out over the water straight ahead?" Ross looked and could see it about a mile away. "Well," the man said, "that is Bethel."

As they drew closer it became apparent that Bethel was simply a church, built right over the water and sitting some way out from a very wild little key. There was no town and, more astonishing to Ross, not even any cultivated land nearby. Ross stared in amazement at the shack projecting up out of the water, wondering why they would build a church with no connection to land. He looked all around and, seeing no houses, asked, "Where do the members live?"

The boatmen explained that the members lived on various islands as well as on the mainland. They pointed as they told him that some lived as far away as ten or fifteen miles and all traveled by canoe. For this reason the church was on the water so they could tie their boats to the piling. The water around the church was their parking lot.

After making the boat fast, the two men helped Ross climb out and up onto a porch built all the way around the church. They handed over his luggage and told him they would go home to get their families and bring them back to the meeting.

They left Ross on the porch, and he watched the canoe grow smaller in the distance and finally disappear from sight. Never had he felt more alone. Baboons screamed from the trees on the nearby island, strange birds called, and uncomfortably close, he heard the heavy body of a crocodile slide into the water. Those intermittent sounds served to accent the brooding silence that hung in the heavy air. The world Ross had left behind seemed like something he had only dreamed about or read about in a book.

He decided to shave while waiting for the congregation to arrive, so he dipped his brush in the salt water of the lagoon and lathered up. He was rinsing off his face when he saw a canoe bounding over the waves toward him. It was too early for the meeting, and he had no way of knowing who it was, so he watched warily as it drew up. To his relief he saw it was a man and woman with friendly smiles. "Are you thirsty?" the man called out.

"I surely am," he shouted back. After the long wait in the heat at Bocas, the canoe ride, and now another wait, Ross was very thirsty and had been longing desperately for a drink of water. The couple produced two coconuts, cut them open, and Ross had a refreshing drink of the thirst-quenching coconut water. Then the two pulled away, saying, "We have to get our children ready, and we will all be back for the service. We live over there." They pointed at one of the keys.

The couple was hardly out of sight when another canoe drew up and a woman and her teenage son hauled out a basket with lunch for the pastor. Ross thanked them, and they paddled away. He ate and then relaxed in the shade after his meal and had just dozed off when something woke him up. Looking out across the water, he saw canoes in all directions coming to church. As each family arrived, they fastened the painter and climbed up onto the porch to enter the church. Soon there was very little parking space left as the canoes were tied all around the church. The sanctuary was filled with a crowd eager to hear the message.

The old familiar hymns rang out across the waters and echoed back. The words took on a special significance in this place. "Peace, be still" had new meaning, and afterwards, whenever he heard the old hymn "Master, the Tempest Is Raging!" he thought of Bethel, where the wind and the waves had real meaning. "The billows are tossing high! / The sky is o'er-shadowed with blackness; / No shelter or help is nigh; / . . . Peace, be still! / . . . Peace, be still!"

Ross's message for that day was about the mission of the church. When he mentioned the Ingathering campaign soon to be launched, the members assured him they would raise the goal the conference had set for them. *How can this be?* Ross wondered as he studied the group before him, none of them rich or even what would be called comfortably well off in the United States. Not one of them had a steady job or owned anything but a thatched hut, a dugout canoe, and maybe a little plot of land. He knew there were no towns nearby and that their neighbors had no more wealth than they. He looked out of the window at the distant keys and asked, "Where do you go to solicit?"

Brother Riley, the local elder, stood up and said, "You see, Elder, we go down the coast to a coconut plantation, a big plantation. We all meet at the church on a certain morning early, and we go together and stay all day. We tell them about Jesus and ask for help to support the work of the church. People are interested and listen to the message and give what they can. We went out last year after Sister Sype wrote to us, and we will go again this year." He turned around to the group and smiled, a slow smile that began in the wrinkles around his eyes in his lean face. Heads were nodding, and Ross heard "Amens" all around.

The sun was sinking in the west as the service drew to a close with the old beloved hymn, "Blest Be the Tie That Binds." The rich, clear voices blending together without the aid of a piano sang the familiar words, "When we asunder part, / It gives us inward pain; / But we shall still be joined in heart, / And hope to meet again."

After the benediction darkness came suddenly, and someone lit a lamp. Ross tucked his Bible under his arm and walked to the door as everyone filed out. They shook hands warmly, thanked him for the sermon, and then with one accord they turned around and walked back to their seats. Brother Riley stood up and announced that there would be another sermon immediately.

Stunned by this request, Ross stammered in unbelief, "But . . . but won't you get tired?"

The crinkled smile again lighted up the good brother's simple, earnest face as he exclaimed, "Oh, no, Elder Sype. We don't have a minister here often, and we never get tired of hearing about Jesus."

Looking out at the darkness that stretched around them on all sides, Ross asked, "But how will you get home in the dark? I know some of you have come as far as thirteen or fourteen miles."

One of the deacons spoke up, "Don't worry about that, Elder. God wants us here, and He will see that we get home safely."

So the pastor launched into the second sermon, again they sang "Blest Be the Tie That Binds," and now it was really dark, for there was no moon. Ross had been invited to go home with Brother Riley, and he felt some apprehension as they were preparing to leave, realizing that he would have another ride in a canoe, this time in the dark. He recalled that the men who had brought him there told him the elder lived fourteen miles away. By now the wind had risen and the waves were making smart little slapping sounds against the pilings. He could imagine whitecaps forming out on the Chiriqui Lagoon, while below in the dark there awaited him a very small dugout canoe.

But there was no other way, so he let himself down into the tiny boat and was soon underway with Brother Riley and his wife. Since the wind was blowing briskly, the elder hoisted a sail, and they flew along. But even with the sail it seemed like a long fourteen miles in that little canoe on the wild, dark waters. They reached Brother Riley's house at last, a thatched hut built high over the water. The boat sailed in under the house, and the elder tied it up. To get up into the house, they climbed the familiar jungle ladder, a notched log.

That night Ross slept as the natives slept, as jungle beasts slept, close to the water and the trees and the life that goes on there. Monkeys and baboons screamed and night birds called, and now and then there was an ominous growl. No modern man had interfered here yet, and ecology took care of itself.

The next day Brother Riley took Ross almost fifteen miles by canoe up the coast to Almirante, where he was to meet J. P. Greene. J. P. had come down from Guabito on a little fruit company train. The two of them planned to visit remote and out-of-the-way churches in the area, some of them miles from the railroad and reachable only by a narrow footpath.

After holding meetings in several of these isolated places, the two missionaries went on to Guabito, where they ingathered in the United Fruit Company offices. They spent that weekend at San San Durui, several miles into dense jungle from Guabito. A narrow winding footpath, packed hard from years of barefoot travel, led to the church itself, built over a low-lying swampy place and set six feet above ground on pilings. A walkway built of native logs led from the path to the church, and then the walk was built around to the back of the building. A room they called the Prophet's Room was reserved for the visiting workers. Ross and J. P. spent the Sabbath there.

Next morning they set out toward the border to cross into Costa Rica and visit an isolated family. While at the family's home, Ross learned that the Sinclair Oil Company had a large crew of men camped out in the hills twenty miles away, prospecting for oil. Since these men were all Americans and well-paid technicians, Ross decided to go out and talk to them about the mission work and solicit them for Ingathering. He knew getting out there would be difficult, for twenty jungle miles is not like twenty miles in the United States, but he was determined to give it a try.

After J. P. had left to go back to the Isthmus, Ross boarded the train and took it to where a branch line led to the camp, fifteen miles into the bush. This stretch was not strong enough to carry trains so was reached by hand-cars and gasoline-powered small cars. When he reached the end of that line, he stopped where some natives were working on the tracks. Glad for a chance to talk with someone, they stopped and leaned on their picks and shovels. "Can you tell me how to get out to the camp?" he asked.

They had a little conference among themselves, and then the spokesman replied, "You have to get permission to go to the camp." He pointed at a little shack and added, "The boss man is there in his office. You have to see him."

The boss was surprised to see another white man at his door and, after offering Ross water to drink and some refreshing tropical fruit, he asked, "What can I do for you?"

Ross told him about the work they were doing in that country and explained the Ingathering campaign. "We are bringing the message of God to isolated people, and now we are giving our friends the opportunity to assist us in this work. I wonder if you wouldn't like to help out and also allow me to go out to the camp and talk to the men out there."

The boss took out his billfold and gave a good offering. He said, "I will be glad to help you in any way I can, but the next handcar won't go out to the camp until tomorrow afternoon. You would have to stay here all night and sleep on a crude bunk." Looking at Ross's suit and shoes, he laughed in an apologetic way and added, "I doubt if you care to go through all that."

"I would love to stay, if you will let me. Don't worry. I am used to roughing it," Ross replied, looking down at his clothing. "They expect you to dress this way if you are a pastor, even out in the bush."

"You are welcome to stay. It's not the Ritz, but you can have that bunk over there, and I'll fix us up some supper. I'm not a great cook, but I'm not too bad."

The next afternoon Ross rode along with an American employee of the oil company at the helm of a little handcar making its way through fifteen miles of virgin forest. When they arrived at camp, the men were just coming in from work, and the oil company worker introduced Ross to them as a minister. The boss was congenial, and the men were happy to have someone new to talk with. That night they asked him to tell some of his missionary experiences while they were relaxing in the dining hall. They were truly interested and listened like children as he told them about Bethel, Bocas del Toro, and some of the remote jungle churches as well as the people who had found God there.

The next morning at breakfast the boss said, "Now, Reverend, it is time for you to tell us just why you came out here." The men turned expectant faces toward Ross as he stood up to explain his mission and introduce the Ingathering work. He then asked for freewill offerings. They were impressed with the work and the message. Willing and eager to help, they peeled off five, ten, and even twenty-dollar bills. They wished him well before going back to work, and Ross left with a tidy sum for missions and a warm spot in his heart for the employees of Sinclair Oil Company.

Chapter 12
Adventures in Costa Rica

The cities of Costa Rica are located in the great mountainous interior. At two thousand feet above sea level, the valleys are rich and the climate almost ideal. The people are more purely Castilian Spanish than in any other part of Central America. It was there in the mountains that the Central American missionaries, worn from dealing with the tropical lowlands, went on vacation. After months of the debilitating climate of the coastal region, Ross, exhausted from frequent malarial attacks, needed a respite from the heat and humidity. Added to that, Gertrude's pregnancy had made her feel especially listless.

Before they left for vacation, the conference committee needed to find a replacement for Gertrude as home missionary secretary (personal ministries). They were pleased with the work she had done, but now that she was pregnant and wouldn't be able to travel as widely, she would need to be replaced by someone who could keep in touch with the churches. When the committee met, they elected Ross to that position, so with that settled, Ross and Gertrude set off for Costa Rica, along with Marie and J. P. Greene, who were also beginning to feel listless from the climate.

The two couples took a boat to Port Limón and then boarded a train for San José. The trip by rail was an exhilarating experience on a route that was then called one of the wonders of the world. The track wound through the jungle and then began the climb into the mountains. Traversing deep gorges, climbing steep mountains, crossing frothing rivers, the train carried them into the scenic highlands. Their spirits soared, and they were revived by the cool air up above the steaming tropics.

Two great volcanoes dominate that general area. Irazú is the highest and was active, while Poás was called semiactive, with a boiling pool in the crater but no smoke ascending from it. The vacationers decided that no trip to Costa Rica would be complete without a view of a volcano, so they decided to make the climb to Poás. For the first leg of the journey they boarded a train taking them to Alajuela. Here they hired an ox cart to carry them and their camping equipment to the small town of San Pedro, where they stayed the night.

Next morning the men went out early to make arrangements for the climb to Mount Poás. Soon they returned and strode eagerly into camp, and Ross announced in a loud, cheerful voice, "Everybody ready for today? We make the rest of the way on horseback!"

Each of them beamed at the prospect of a ride in such lovely surrounding, except Marie, who turned pale and looked at Ross beseechingly as she said weakly, "Horses! You mean we have to ride horses?"

"Of course. It's a very steep climb and rocky. Everybody takes horses. You get them at a stable in the village," Ross explained.

"What's wrong, Marie?" Gertrude asked. "You aren't afraid of horses, are you?"

"Yes, I am. I know it sounds silly, but when I was little a horse threw me, and I have never ridden since."

J. P. put his arm around his wife and said, "Honey, these horses don't have enough energy to shake off a fly. They are overworked and underfed. The main problem with them is to keep them from stopping."

"Isn't there some other way?" Marie implored.

"Afraid not," J. P. answered, giving her a little squeeze, "Come on now. Don't spoil our trip. There is nothing to be afraid of. Those horses go on that trail every day and are well-trained. Little children ride them."

"Children don't have sense enough to be afraid," Marie sniffed, "but if that is the only way to go, I'll try."

"Atta girl," cheered Gertrude. "Remember that even I, who am in a 'delicate condition,' am going to ride."

When they got to the stable, a groom saddled up four small, thin horses and led them out. J. P. pointed out to Marie how small they were, really no more than ponies, and how docile, dull even, as they stood tied to the rail, heads drooping. "We'll let Marie take first pick," Ross offered. "Which one do you want, Marie?" She pointed to a sorry-looking little bay dozing in the morning sun, not even switching his tail to drive the flies away. "I'll take that one," she decided. "He looks kind of sick."

They started up the trail single file, with Marie bringing up the rear, clutching the reins in one hand and the saddle horn in the other. Right from the start the little bay sensed her fear and at the first turn, while the others went around a clump of trees, it tried to scrape her off by going through them. "Whoa, help, help!" she cried, tugging on the reigns with one hand and fending off the branches with the other. J. P. hurried to her rescue and led her horse back onto the trail.

They began a steep climb with a series of switchbacks. Some of the turns led up to the edge of a crevasse where, as J. P. told them cheerfully, if you were inclined to vertigo it was best not to look down. Marie's horse carried her quietly and with no incident for several miles, but then without warning he walked a little faster up to an overhang and stopped abruptly, almost pitching her from the saddle. Petrified with fear, she looked down into the abyss while the horse stiffened under her, pretending he had seen some terror in the bushes. Again the party was stopped by a faint cry for help, and J. P. rode back to find Marie sitting on the ground plucking aimlessly at the grass while the little bay, with reins dragging, was eating blissfully nearby. Marie looked defiantly at J. P. and said, "Just go on without me. I won't get back on. He tried to throw me over the cliff." She buried her face in her hands and burst into tears.

Gertrude brought out some fruit and water, and they sat in the shade and relaxed while the starved little horses ate the grass around them. Then J. P. tied a long rope to Marie's horse and, for the rest of the ride, led it along. The little bay followed quietly. As long as Marie didn't try to guide it, it didn't pull any more tricks.

When the group got to the top, they looked inside the volcano and admired the awe-inspiring view. The part Marie never forgot was how J. P. had to lead that ornery little bay horse every step of the way.

The day sped by and then the friends, refreshed by the stay in Costa Rica, found it was time to go back to work. Gertrude returned to Colón with the Greenes, while Ross stayed on to visit the English-speaking churches in the lowland banana country. Upon his return to Port Limón after this tour, he found another assignment awaiting him.

A young French girl, Melba, who was attending school in Port Limón, Costa Rica, needed someone to escort her home to Bocas del Toro. The girl lived with her brother, who was married to a Bay Island native woman and was the foreman of a plantation. Melba was a deeply spiritual girl, and her brother was concerned about her future in Bocas, so he determined to send her to Port Limón to attend a mission school. Getting her back and forth from school, however, was an almost overwhelming problem. In the fall Jacob Osborne had escorted her from Bocas to Port Limón. He found the whole journey to be primitive, dangerous, and tedious. Not only were the hazards of travel a worry, but also there was the fear that something could happen to the young lady. Now that it was vacation time again and she needed to travel back home to Bocas, Ross was assigned to accompany her on the return trip.

Out at the school Ross learned when Melba would be ready to leave for her vacation, and then he began to map out the trip. The first leg of the trek would be in a motorboat from Port Limón, so on the appointed day at four o'clock in the morning. Ross and Melba were waiting at the dock in the darkness for the boat. Melba was a beautiful young woman of sixteen with dark eyes and hair that hung down her back. At first almost painfully shy, she replied to Ross's attempts at conversation with monosyllables. As they talked she began to relax and confided that she wanted to be a teacher. She liked school very much and did not look forward to vacation in Bocas. "It is hard to find nice friends," she explained. "They come to my house and coax me to go to the dance and the theater."

"What do you tell them?" Ross asked.

"I tell them it is no place for a Christian. But one time last summer when I had nothing to do, I gave in and went to the motion picture theater with some girls. I soon found out it was not a picture for a Christian to be looking at. I sat for a while and then I felt so guilty I began to perspire. The sweat was running off me, and I whispered to one of my friends, 'It's too hot for me in here' and I got out of there." She paused and shook her head at the memory and added with a laugh, "It was too hot for me but in a different way than they thought."

Four o'clock passed but no boat appeared, and at last a man came out and shouted, "The boat is gone!"

"How can that be?" asked Ross, "I was told it left at four."

"There was a storm at sea," the rather excited young man explained, waving his arms about. "A boat out there requested help, so they sent this boat to help them." Shrugging his shoulders, he added that they would let him know when the vessel came in.

There was nothing for the travelers to do but return to the school and wait. Later in the day one of the men came and said, "Elder, I know why you missed that boat this morning. That was a bad storm out there, and they believe the boat that was in trouble and the rescue boat are both lost. If you had been on that boat, you would have gone down with the others. Some other passengers were waiting for the boat you were to take, so they would have been lost too."

Ross had a long time to think about the sequence of events that prevented their being aboard that ill-fated craft, and he saw more clearly than ever how God was leading in his life. He offered a prayer of thanks for this delay, although he had been quite impatient to get home as he had received word that Gertrude was not well.

Another vessel had to be rigged up, so it was not until late in the morning that they set sail for Gandoca. According to the schedule, a little horse-drawn car on a tiny track would meet them at this port and take them to the Sixaola River, where they would board a boat bound for Guabito. At Guabito they would ride on a train for the rest of the trip.

Late that evening they landed at Gandoca, which Ross presumed was a small town, but to his amazement the boat stopped at a landing place on a lonely coast without even a dock. All he could see in the clearing were two dingy thatched huts surrounded by trees that pressed menacingly close. Since there was no wharf, the passengers were carried to shore by two men, their muscles rippling under gleaming skin. The boat pulled away, leaving Ross and Melba alone in the growing darkness with two natives who appeared sullen and arrogant. To add to Ross's distress, he could not help seeing the looks the men cast at the beautiful Melba. He turned to the two and asked, "How do we get to Guabito?"

"A horse-drawn car will take you over to the Sixaola River, where you will get a vessel," one of the men answered.

"What time does the car leave?"

"It has already left. You will have to spend the night here," replied the man, giving Melba a long, level look.

The girl didn't raise her eyes but shifted uncomfortably at this news. With some apprehension, Ross asked, "Where will we stay?"

"Over there in that hut. Me and my buddy stay in this one," the man answered, pointing to the nearest hovel.

The jungle night was coming down, and noises from the bush were very loud in that great and solemn darkness. Ross led the way to the shelter, feeling a premonition of dread as the full impact of his position came to him. Why hadn't he gotten more details about the trip? Here he was, completely cut off from civilization with two ruthless-looking men. His responsibility for Melba's safety haunted him as he realized that both their lives were in jeopardy, hers even more than his. In this dark hour he knew their only hope was in the Almighty, and he prayed as they walked to the hut.

"Are you afraid, Melba?" he asked as they entered the low doorway.

"Not as long as I am with you, Elder," she whispered, "but when I first saw those men I . . . I was a little afraid."

Her confidence overwhelmed him as he considered their vulnerability and the dangers all around, not only from their companions but from the jungle itself, housed as they were in this miserable little shack while outside were beasts of prey and great snakes. Ross prayed for God to give him the strength that Melba thought he had. Putting his bag on the floor, he dug around and brought out a candle and some matches. After lighting the candle, he found a few sandwiches, some fruit, and a canteen of water. They surveyed the inside of the shelter by the flickering light of the candle as they ate.

Ross always carried a mosquito net and a hammock with him, so he hung up the hammock and said, "Melba, you take the hammock, and I will take the net and sleep on the porch. But first let's have prayer and ask the Lord to shield us from harm."

He pushed a bench in front of the door to bar entrance in case one of the men got any ideas in the night, hung the mosquito netting over the bench, crawled under it, and tried to sleep. The girl got into the hammock and was soon fast asleep, but Ross spent a restless night of prayerful vigilance. When he did drift off to sleep on his hard bed, he would awaken in a sweat of fear at the slightest noise. The long night passed slowly as he watched the stars in their orbit and listened to the voice of the jungle around him. There was no sound from the other hut, and Melba slept on.

At last the sun came up, pushing aside the darkness and with it the gloom and dread of the night. There was a freshness in the air, and birds were singing. The two men were kneeling before a fire, and Ross and Melba could smell food cooking. The men didn't seem so sinister now in the morning light, and when they waved and called out a greeting, the travelers went over to the fire where they were broiling two fish, freshly caught in the river. "Good fish," one of the men said. "Have some. You must be hungry too." Ross and Melba thanked them and shared the fresh, delicious fish, standing around the fire with the two men.

While they ate Ross said, "Did you know that one time Jesus cooked fish for the disciples' breakfast?" The men turned toward him with interest, so he continued. "After the Crucifixion, Jesus had come back to visit His friends. Peter and six of the others—James, John, Thomas, Nathaniel, and two others had gone out in a boat and fished all night but hadn't caught anything. As dawn began to break, the fishermen noticed a man standing on the shore. Who could it be? they wondered. He called out to them, 'Do you have any fish?' They said they didn't have any. Again the man called to them, 'Cast the net on the right side of the boat and you will find fish.' So they cast the net and caught so many fish, they could not haul the net in. Then John recognized the stranger. 'It is the Lord!' he whispered to Peter, so they all leaped out of the boat and dragged the net full of fish to shore. Then they smelled something good, just like Melba and I did this morning, because Jesus had made a fire and was broiling fish for their breakfast."

The men listened to the story, and then they began to talk with Ross like old friends. Soon the car arrived to take Ross and Melba to the Sixaola River. An old horse pulled the car slowly up a hill and down into the valley to the river, where a motor boat was waiting to take them to Guabito, a primitive little town but a metropolis compared to Gandoca. At Guabito they boarded a train for Bocas, and soon Melba was safely home.

Ross then took a train for Almirante and from there a small boat to Colón, where Gertrude was anxiously waiting for him as the baby's birth was imminent. He was able to stay home for several months and catch up on his office work, so he was present on August 1, 1921, when little Minita arrived. She was named after her grandmothers, both named Minnie. Minita means "Little Minnie" in Spanish. Ross loved being with Gertrude and this little girl who had brown eyes like his own and tiny hands that clung to his finger so tightly. He wanted to stay there for a long time, but other boats were sailing, and he would be aboard one of them.

Chapter 13
Storm at Sea

As Ross sat at his desk in Colón on a September morning, a voice suddenly broke the silence like the booming of surf. "Hello, Elder Sype. Are you ready for your trip to San Andrés and Providence?"

"Captain Archbold!" he exclaimed, leaping to his feet and extending his hand. "I am delighted to see you. When are you sailing?"

"The ship is in port now in Colón, and we set sail this afternoon," the captain replied, looking somehow out of place in the little office, standing as he did with feet far apart as if he expected the floor to move beneath him. His eyes, which had taken on the quality of sea and sky, seemed always to be searching far horizons. Ross knew this was not a man to be kept waiting, so he promised to be at the dock at one o'clock.

Ross viewed the proposed trip with mixed feelings. He wanted to spend more time at home with Gertrude and little Minita, but on the other hand he was eager to visit those islands and felt fortunate to be sailing with Captain Archbold. The captain, a descendent of one of the original Archbolds on Old Providence Island, had followed the sea since he was a boy and was now the owner of a choice sailing vessel. In addition, he was also the *alcalde*, or ruler, of the island and the elder of the Adventist church there.

The two Colombian islands were part of the vast Inter-American mission field. The two islands had always been regarded as an enigma, lying in splendid isolation two hundred and fifty miles from Panama in the blue waters of the Caribbean. Geographically the two are neighbors, but each is forever alone, mysterious, and inscrutable. Although they belong to the country of

Colombia, both are English-speaking, and although they are twins in that lonely, boundless sea, they are a sharp contrast in appearance. San Andrés is comparatively level, while Old Providence is simply the tops of mountains thrust up out of the sea. Besides the obvious physical difference, each has an entirely different cultural background.

The history of San Andrés goes back to the days when the British lived there and worked the land with slaves. When all bondsmen were freed in the British West Indies, the British themselves deserted the island and left it to their slaves. The descendents of those slaves occupy the island today. At first in their newfound freedom on this tropical island, where the living was easy, the former slaves gave themselves over to wickedness and debauchery. They were completely irreligious until some missionaries arrived. The missionaries worked among them and made gradual inroads until the people, who were slaves first to men and then to evil, began to change and accept Christianity. At the time Ross visited the island, he found a flourishing church and school.

The first inhabitants of San Andrés' sister island, Old Providence Island, were also Englishmen, but these were English sailors for the most part who, under circumstances long forgotten or best unremembered, had jumped ship. A few had English wives but most of them married women from the Central American mainland. Ross found three names prominent among the descendents there—Archbold, Newbold, and Robinson. Because of the terrain of this island there was little or no agriculture, so the men were all seamen, very good sailors who operated schooners plying the surrounding waters and visiting all the ports of Central America. It was the Old Providence vessels that carried passengers to and from the islands.

That afternoon Ross boarded the sailboat and set off for the islands in good weather. Sitting on deck, he watched the prow of the boat cutting through the waves and reveled in the ship's roll, the cool spray of salt water, and the caress of the breeze. After an enjoyable voyage, he saw the island appear on the horizon. Escorted by flocks of sea birds wheeling overhead, the boat drew up to the landing on the south end of the island, where one of the villages stood. The other village at the north end was the capital and the residence of the Colombian officials, the only Spanish-speaking people of the island.

Ross planned to stay and work on San Andrés for two or three weeks and then sail to Old Providence with Captain Archbold on his next voyage. Because there were no taxis, he walked the three miles to the church after making arrangements for his baggage to be sent on by mule. He spent a busy three weeks holding meetings and visiting the members on the island. It was nine miles long and two or three miles wide, and he covered most of it on foot. Since there were few problems to deal with, he spent the time with spiritual revival. It was a refreshing sojourn. In his walks back and forth, Ross often met natives leading mules loaded down with coconuts, carrying them to the little port to be shipped to England and America. The sacks were balanced on each side, and sometimes a man or boy would be riding as well.

One day a messenger came to the church to report that Captain Archbold was in port and was expecting Ross to sail to Old Providence with him that afternoon. After lunch, he hurried down to the port. Just as he was stepping on the gangplank to board the ship, he heard someone calling him. Looking back, he saw a man running toward the wharf waving his arms and shouting. Almost spent with his effort, the man doubled up to try to catch his breath. "Thank God you're still here, Elder," he gasped.

Recognizing him as a member of the church, Ross asked, "What's wrong, Bill?"

Bill was beginning to breathe easier but was overcome by emotion as he tried to speak. "It's Thomas, John's boy. He fell out of a coconut tree and struck his head. Poor Tommy. There was nothing we could do. He's dead, Elder." He gave a deep sob and paused, turning beseeching eyes upon Ross. "John wants you to have the funeral this afternoon."

"Of course, Bill, I'll go right back with you," Ross assured him. Turning to the captain, he said, "Well, you'll have to sail without me. Please explain to the Providence members. Tell them I'll come on the next boat going that way."

Ross started the long walk with Bill along the trail where, in the happy days of his visit, he had met John and his boys mounted on their sturdy mules carrying loads of coconuts to the port. John was a deacon in the church, a tall, friendly faced man, and his boys had the same frank, pleasant face and friendly smile. But their happiness had come to an end, and it was terribly quiet that day. There was no laughter of children or shouting of men or muffled hoof beats of mules along the dusty path.

Mourners filled the church late that afternoon and sang songs of comfort and hope, and they paid tribute to Tommy. A long procession of family and friends followed the little coffin carried by strong men to the cemetery.

A week went by before another schooner came into port, and Ross arranged to sail to Old Providence on it. As the departure time drew near, Ross saw a very large dark cloud to the north, the direction in which the ship was to go. Some of the men down at the shore looked up to the sky, and one of them said, "Elder, we don't like the look of that cloud. We don't often have a hurricane in these parts, but that sure looks like one." Some of the older men were shaking their heads gravely, and all looked worried. The cloud looked menacing, although those islands are just south of the hurricane belt and were seldom hit. It was true that Old Providence sometimes got the tail end of a hurricane, but they were rarely heard of at San Andrés, as was evidenced by the haphazard way the inhabitants built their homes. The little cabins in the coastal village stood up on small posts several feet from the ground and would never stand up before the fury of a full-blown hurricane.

Unlike most sea captains, who were stalwart, forthright men, the captain of this boat, Captain Dickinson, was a vacillating, uncertain sort who looked up at the clouds and listened to the men milling about on shore and did not know whether he should sail or not. He went to the owner of the boat, who was sailing with them, and asked his advice. He replied, "Captain, that is what I hired you for. When you say 'sail,' we will sail."

The shilly-shallying skipper paced up and down, again studied the ugly clouds massing in the north, again conferred with the men on shore, and then, with an air of desperation, asked Ross what he thought. "Actually, Captain," Ross replied, "I'm new to the islands and I don't know what those clouds signify, but I am ready to sail whenever you say so."

An old man in rumpled clothes, with a wad of chewing tobacco resting in his cheek, walked up with the rolling gait of a seasoned sailor. He turned out to be a retired sea captain who was booking passage for Old Providence on the boat. He listened to the debate about whether to sail or not and cast a rheumy eye at the clouds. He said loudly, "Why, captain, I am surprised at you being afraid of that cloud. I sailed these waters many years and a little cloud like that never stopped me." He shot a stream of brown tobacco juice at a rock with some expertise, wiped his mouth with the back of his hand, and looked each man in the eye with a sort of defiance. At these brave words the captain called the sailors to haul up the anchor, and they set sail.

They got under way with full sails and a good breeze, and it looked as if it would be a pleasant, quick trip. Ross, who was feeling the effects of the vigorous four weeks he had put in on San Andrés, decided to go below and rest for a while.

Lulled by the long swells of the Caribbean and the forward motion of the boat, Ross had fallen into the deep sleep of the young and weary. He dreamed then, and in his dream he was back home in Iowa. His mother stood before him wearing her hat and coat with her Bible under one arm, and she pulled on her gloves as he had seen her do many times. It was all so clear—the round, unsmiling face, the brown snapping eyes, the long, dark hair drawn back in a knot, the short stocky figure. She was telling him to hitch the team to the sleigh because they had a meeting in Lake City. Next they were driving across the prairie when suddenly a blizzard overtook them. The horses labored through the snow, trying to pull the sleigh. It swayed and bucked as they hit the drifts that formed endlessly across the flat landscape. Then the sleigh tipped over, and the horses were plunging into the darkness, out of control.

The next thing Ross knew, he was on the floor shouting, "Whoa, whoa! Mother, where are you?" He tried to get up, but the floor would not hold still, and after much effort he managed to grab hold of something solid and pull himself to a sitting position. Dazed and bewildered, he looked around and tried to remember where he was. It came back to him—the schooner, the threatening skies, the huge Caribbean. And he knew it was the ship bucking the waves, for obviously the feared storm had struck.

He crawled up on deck and could see sheets of driving water, the pitching boat, the crew making desperate attempts to keep her afloat and headed in the right direction. The little craft twisted and rolled, diving down in the trough of a giant wave and then riding the crest up and up to dive down again with sickening speed. It was like riding on a giant roller coaster running out of control. Ducking back inside the cabin, Ross careened across the hold, striking another passenger before he managed to wedge himself against something solid.

As the storm worsened, the passengers were herded into the cargo deck, crewmen latched the hatch, and they were left there to suffer out the storm. The small hold, dank and fetid, was crammed with people, vomiting and retching, made sick by the motion of the boat as it was tossed about in the storm. The sounds of the storm added to the terror—the creaking of the ship as she wallowed in the high seas; the roar of the wind; and the moans, groans, curses, and prayers of frightened people.

"Ore por nosotros, Pastor" ("Pray for us, Pastor"), a small, dark woman begged, clutching Ross's sleeve with thin, desperate hands. Ross was not easily frightened, but as he looked into the eyes of the woman asking him to pray, he felt a despair he had never experienced before. His thoughts went to his wife and baby girl back in Colón, and he wondered if he would ever see them again. He pictured Gertrude getting the news of his drowning, holding little Minita and sobbing. Was God going to let his career and his dreams end here?

His mind flashed back in time to the little Iowa farm of his boyhood. He recalled overhearing his father praying aloud for him in the barn, and then later his conversion at Oak Park Academy and his determination to dedicate his life to the Lord's work. He relived meeting the lovely Gertrude, with her vibrant personality and steadfast character. And also there was his mother, praying for him and giving him once more, across the miles, her special brand of courage. The Lord had seen him through countless perils—ugly mobs, the jungle with its seen and unseen dangers, the attacks of malaria he had weathered—and he could not think that God would forsake him now. His eyes closed and his lips moved as he prayed, "Dear Lord, make me worthy of Your blessings and protection. If it is Your will, please let me see Gertrude and little Minita again. I'll never cease to serve You. Thank You for answering my prayer."

"¡Ore por nosotros!" came the voice again, and he opened his eyes to see the desperate face again, the thin hands shaking his arm.

"Sí, Señora, yo estoy orando" ("Yes, Sister, I am praying"), he answered, trying to make himself heard above the roar of the storm. He stood up, braced himself against the wall, and preached one of his best sermons— short, pointed, and to an audience that was most receptive. "God is going to see us through this safely, and when you reach land, don't forget Him."

The hold became quiet. Men stopped cursing, and women drew around him holding their babies close. *"Sí, Pastor,"* they said and prayed softly in Spanish.

Gradually, the wind died down and the seas became less threatening. The boat was still wallowing in the high seas off the lee of Old Providence, but the worst was over, and the crew opened the hatch, letting the passengers out into the fresh air. Skinny, wiry little men needing a shave and grim, frightened women and an endless parade of children of all ages trooped out and stood on deck, chattering like a flock of bedraggled sparrows.

Just then they heard the captain shout to the sailors that the boat was almost on the rocks. Again the pastor prayed, his head bowed and the ragged cluster of passengers turning toward him in this new terror. *Surely,* he thought, *God didn't bring us through that harrowing experience only to be dashed to pieces on jagged rocks.* The sailors fell to and, with excited shouts and gestures, delicately maneuvered the vessel through a pass between two gigantic rocks, and then to the relief of everyone, they sailed at last into the quiet, tranquil waters along the coast of the island of Old Providence.

After the storm there was great quiet. The shining trees along the shore hung limp as if spent. Long combers slapped playfully at the beach pounded smooth as a floor. A cloudless sky bent over a languid sea. Birds began to sing and search wildly for food.

Since life on Old Providence revolved around the sea and shipping, most of the men were sailors or in some way connected to shipping. The little island—bare, rugged, and lonely—projects out of the Caribbean fifty miles from her nearest neighbor and almost one hundred and fifty miles from the mainland. She was inhabited by people who lived in their own small world, in an isolation unknown on the great continents that lay beyond her horizons. There were few changes in their day-to-day lives. Every day they watched the sun came up out of the sea and go down into the sea. Not surprisingly, every boy longed for the day when he could sail out across the sea, and the arrival of any ship was talked about for days. Although there were no telephones, there was no need for them, for news traveled swiftly. When a ship was sighted, all the inhabitants seemed to know at once.

Captain Dickinson's boat sailed toward the docks to be met by the entire population of the island waiting on the shore. When the ship docked, several of the passengers knelt to kiss the ground and look with new appreciation on this island, blue and gold and limpid with the white sand, the ring of coconut palms, and the air of timelessness those islands seemed to exude.

Ross stepped off the ship with thanksgiving in his heart for his safety, but he could not help looking ruefully at his nice white suit showing the wear and tear of the storm. When he tried to rub off some of the dirt, he only made a smudge, and the Panama hat he had been wearing was crushed beyond help. The shoes that were shiny and new when he left home now gave off a sad little squish at each step.

The church members welcomed Ross and asked excitedly, almost in unison, "Where is Captain Archbold?"

Astonished at this question, he answered, "Why, isn't he here? He left San Andrés a week ago."

At this disquieting report the group at the landing looked at one another in numb disbelief. Mrs. Archbold, who had been first in line to greet Ross, turned pale. A young woman whose sweetheart had been one of the sailors fainted, and children began to cry. A lost ship was their worst nightmare, for they knew how frail the boats were and how powerful the sea. They lived in the shadow of that dark day, and now they had come face to face with it—a missing ship, a captain and crew apparently lost.

Silent in their apprehension and fear, they clustered around the pastor for comfort. He tried to reassure them in the face of their despair. "Remember that Captain Archbold is an expert seaman, and since he also is a servant of our great God, I can't help but believe he is safe somewhere," he said, looking at the grieving faces. "Remember all things are possible with God, and even if the ship went down, the captain and his crew might have been picked up by another boat and are probably alive on a foreign shore. Come, let's go to the church and have a special prayer meeting for Captain Archbold and his crew."

His words had a hollow ring, even to him, but they walked to the church, all of the members and many who were not members, now brothers and sisters in a common grief. They met daily for five days and took their petitions, their grief, and their anxieties to the throne of grace. On the fifth day, late in the afternoon, a little boat arrived with the news that Captain Archbold and the entire crew except the cook had been rescued and were in Costa Rica awaiting a boat to take them home. Their schooner had sunk in a sudden storm, and all made it safely to the life boat except the cook, who had been sleeping down in the cabin. Ross realized with a pang that he would have been sharing that cabin with the cook had he gone on the ill-fated ship.

Captain Archbold and the crew came home on a bright and sunny day to the sound of flutes, marred only by the muffled drums that beat for the cook's family mourning their loved one. New stories were added to the roster of sea tales when the men told of their ordeal in the life boat, how they drifted alone for seven days without water and without food except for the few fish they could snare. Some had sunk into lethargy, and some went quite mad and would have jumped overboard to sink beneath the waves if the captain had not been there to stay them by sheer power of mind and trust in God. Many of them owed their very lives to him, for he was captain in every sense of the word.

Spending several weeks on Old Providence, Ross held a series of revival meetings and visited the entire island and its families. He stayed with a New-bold family, and they let him borrow a horse to ride as he traveled from one place to another. Ross appreciated their generosity because this land is the top of a mountain and the terrain is rough. The path from the Newbolds' home to the church led to a high shelf looking down on the sea on one side and looking up a perpendicular cliff on the other. One day just before dark, Ross rode the horse along this narrow path to the church, where he was going to hold an evening meeting. The view was superb with the sun, an arc of red, disappearing on the distant horizon and the water sparkling like diamonds in its lingering rays. Ross soaked in the grandeur and continued to the church.

However, coming back after the service in the dark was not as delightful. It was, in fact, rather terrifying. The horse's hooves kicked pebbles into the abyss below, and he could hear them go down and down and down. At one point he got off to lead the horse, thinking he might feel his way, for in the deep darkness he could see nothing. Then to his great relief he heard someone call his name and saw a light flickering toward him. It was Brother New-bold coming to meet him. *How like the Christian life,* he mused. *No matter how dark and rocky the path, if we have trust in God and faith to keep moving forward, He will come out to meet us with a light.*

Chapter 14
Revolution in Nicaragua

Ross had been traveling in the field for two and half months, and more than anything he wanted to go home. A boat bound for Colón was due the next day, so he was packing his bags and thinking of the joyful reunion with Gertrude and the baby. Bone weary from the weeks of travel, his thoughts turned to home with its simple pleasures. With the word *home* going through his mind like a song, he went to sleep happy that night.

He was quite unprepared for the message that arrived the next morning. Up bright and early, he was getting ready to go down to the dock to board ship and closed his bag with a decisive snap. Bag in one hand, he reached for the doorknob and was startled by a loud knock. Ross opened the door and saw a messenger holding out a letter from the conference president, Max Trummer. Ross read:

Dear Ross,

Since it is getting near Christmas we need someone to go to the Corn Islands and see that the teacher is conducted safely to her home in Bluefields for her two months' vacation. It is also necessary for an ordained minister to officiate at the Communion service there. Since you are the only one available at this time, I would like for you to book passage on the first boat and proceed accordingly.

Sincerely,
Max Trummer

Holding the letter in his hand, Ross stared in stunned disbelief, realizing that the assignment meant delaying the happy reunion with his family. He would again have to deal with the inconveniences and frustrations of travel in a place where timetables were unknown or ignored and in addition were being disrupted by political revolution. He felt anger surge through him at this thoughtless request in view of the fact that he had been traveling for almost three months. Wild thoughts raced through his mind. Should he ignore the order, perhaps burn the note and pretend he had never gotten it? Then a verse from the book of Luke flashed through his mind, something he had heard his mother say when she was evangelizing on the frontier in Wyoming: "No man, having put his hand to the plough, and looking back, is fit for the kingdom of God" (Luke 9:62). Remembering her struggles as she bore up under drought, a sick husband, and indifference and hostility from strangers, he folded the note and began to make preparations to "book passage on the first boat and proceed accordingly."

Ross had found out by then how uncertain and chancy travel was in Central America, and more often than not you would have to take a circuitous route to get to your destination. In this case he had to go to the Corn Islands off the coast of Nicaragua, pick up the teacher, and then proceed to her home at Bluefields, a port in Nicaragua. Since he was right then in Old Providence, he inquired around and found the best way to get to the Corn Islands was to go back to San Andrés, for a captain there made it a business to sail from San Andrés to Bluefields. Once in Bluefields, Ross would have no trouble finding a boat to the Corn Islands, which belong to Nicaragua. It sounded simple, but he had already learned there were few simple solutions.

Ross arrived at San Andrés with no difficulty and spent the week visiting and holding meetings while waiting for passage to Bluefields. The boat scheduled for Bluefields arrived and lay moored in the harbor. The captain sent word ashore that he was not sailing because the revolution in Nicaragua made it unsafe for small boats to land in Bluefields. More slow days passed, and then word came from the captain that they would sail the next day.

Ross went on board and was greeted by the captain, a tense little man whose round, hard eyes burned in his dark face. Giving Ross a tight, forced smile he said, "Now we sail. I got another message that boats are landing in Bluefields. So we will go before they change their minds. Always something happening in Nicaragua." Pacing around the room, he kept taking sips from a little glass. "Soda water," he told Ross and, patting his stomach tenderly, added, "Ulcer."

"It's a relief to be getting under way at last," Ross told him. "I've been waiting here for days."

"You're not afraid then?" the captain asked, raising a quizzical eyebrow.

"Not if you aren't. I am sure they wouldn't hurt me any quicker than they would you."

"That's the trouble," the captain answered, a cryptic little smile tugging at his mouth. "I'm taking you along for protection, because they would just as soon shoot me as look at me, but they would hesitate to shoot an American."

On their way at last, Ross went to his bunk and slept. Early the next morning he was awakened by the captain, who shouted, "There she is, Pastor, Little Corn Island. Great Corn Island where you have to go is just beyond."

"Good," Ross replied drowsily, "how long will it take us to get there?"

"Sorry, but we aren't going to land. I don't dare go ashore in those islands—the revolution, you know. We'll go on to Bluefields. You will have to find a way from there."

Ross went back to bed but was jarred from slumber by another cry from the captain, who whooped, "Hurrah, look, Pastor, everything will be all right! Uncle Sam is here!" and he pointed to a great white ship lying at anchor offshore. He thought it was a United States battleship, but as they drew nearer his hopes were dashed as it turned out to be a United Fruit Company steamer waiting to be allowed to land.

When the ship docked at Bluefields they found the city was under the control of the revolutionary soldiers, who were down at the wharf guarding the buildings. The young revolutionaries were everywhere, a barefoot, ragtag lot, carrying rifles and scowling at anyone who came near. Ross was assured, however, there would not be much trouble or actual danger. The only consequence would be the inconvenience—the red tape for every move he might try to make. With some misgivings he went to a government building to see about getting over to the Corn Islands. A man with a long thin face like a starved pony sat at the desk, and as Ross entered he raised mournful eyes and nodded.

"Good morning, *Señor,*" Ross greeted him. "I would like to get over to the Corn Islands and wondered if you—"

"Corn Islands!" the official interrupted in barely passable English as he threw up his head and snorted. "You might as well ask to go to the moon, *Señor.*"

"Isn't there some way? I must get over there."

"Why the Corn Islands of all places?"

Ross introduced himself and explained that the teacher on Great Corn Island, a young lady, must be escorted to her home in Bluefields, and that he, an American minister, was assigned to this task. He assured the man it was not a pleasure trip, nor was he out for adventure.

Sitting back in his chair, the official put his fingers together and pursed his lips importantly. "Very few boats are going over there, very few," he said slowly. "And even if you do find one, you will have to have a Nicaraguan passport as well as other papers authorizing you to go. All of this will take time—time."

Exhausted and frustrated by the delay, Ross walked over to the window and stared out into the street. His shoulders sagged as he pondered his situation. He had really hit a brick wall this time. There had to be some way he could get the papers. After all, he was on business for the Lord.

"Mr. Sype."

Hearing his name called, Ross turned and saw the man at the desk motioning to him. He shuffled through some papers, made a few notes with a squeaky pen, and then said in his thick accent, "Since you are an American missionary, I think I can fix it up so you can be on your way this afternoon." He looked at his watch and continued. "It's noon now. A boat is leaving in about an hour, so I'm sending word to them to reserve a place for you. I'll also give you a pass that will get you by the soldiers."

Ross shook the man's hand and said, "Thank you. God will bless you."

In a short time he was on board waiting to sail, but before they were under way, shots rang out down by the dock. People dived for cover while the revolutionary soldiers scattered in all directions. Government troops from Managua had arrived and taken over the town. Not a shot was fired by the revolutionaries. They did not have an army strong enough to force a showdown, so they turned and fled. The government troops stood guard, and the insurgents bolted for the hills to regroup.

Now that the government had dispelled the rebels and was back in control, Ross thought there would be no more trouble. At long last he could get over to Great Corn Island, pick up the teacher, deliver her to her home, and be on his way. He turned to a passenger who stood near him and said, "Now I have seen a *coup d'etat*. Didn't amount to much, did it?"

"Goes on all the time," the man said, shrugging his shoulders. "First one in control and then the other. That's Central American politics for you." Then he stiffened and, putting a hand on Ross's arm, whispered, "See that man dressed in white coming out of that stateroom over there? He's a lawyer. And he's the leader of the revolutionaries."

Ross watched with interest as the tall, slightly stooped man with a long waving moustache walked down the hall. It was impossible to see his face under the wide-brimmed hat pulled low over his forehead. Flanked by three other men walking a little behind, he seemed to be deep in thought. The other passengers watched them with covered eyes until they disappeared.

"Think he will cause any trouble?" Ross asked anxiously.

"I'm not sure. The Corn Islands are loyal to the Managua government," the man replied.

"I hope we aren't held up any longer because of his being on board," Ross said. "I wonder why he is going to the islands."

"He has his reasons," the man answered. "They call him The Fox."

The ship arrived at Great Corn Island without incident, and the captain advised Ross he had better return with him as few boats were running between there and the mainland. Ross spent the Sabbath with the Adventist believers and held their Communion service. After a busy Sabbath, Ross and the teacher went to the dock late on Saturday night, ready to board the boat for home. They walked toward the little office expecting to pick up their landing papers for Bluefields but found no one there except the ship's captain and The Fox, the revolutionary lawyer, and a retinue of two young men. Ross looked around and asked, "Where is the postmaster? He was going to issue our papers."

One of the young men said the postmaster had left for home hours earlier and could not be reached. Ross looked through the window of the office and saw that it was closed and dark. He and the teacher glanced at each other in dismay. "What are we going to do, Elder Sype?" she asked, twisting her hands nervously.

Ross shrugged helplessly and replied, "I don't know. Where else can we go for the papers this time of night?"

The Fox stepped forward and asked, "Do you need something?"

"Yes, we were supposed to pick up our passports here to get us back to Bluefields, but there is no one here. I don't know what to do."

"We can fix that," the lawyer replied and moved confidently toward the door. "I don't think this door is locked." He walked toward it and turned the knob, and to Ross's amazement it opened. The revolutionary leader sat down at the immigration officer's desk, wrote out a passport for both Ross and the teacher in Spanish, sealed it with his personal seal and handed it to them. "You will not have any more trouble," he assured them and with a slight bow, turned to go.

"How can we thank you?" Ross asked.

"Don't try. I am happy to help you." And he was gone. They never saw him again. Staring at the paper with some disbelief, Ross declared, "Well, I hope it gets us through. Remember the revolutionaries are out of power now."

Knowing something of the government on the island, the teacher said, "It is our only hope. Without it we would be stuck here until who knows when. The captain wants to be off. The one man who could issue our passes has gone to bed, and no one else could do it. He is everything on the island— governor, policeman, postman, immigration officer, and everything else."

Ross gave a rueful glance at the papers and said, "Let's be off then. We'll know in the morning when we land at Bluefields."

The next morning the immigration officer came aboard and asked for their papers. In fear and trembling Ross handed him the illegal documents, but the man merely glanced at them and said, *"Bueno, bueno"* as he handed them back.

After seeing the teacher united with her family, Ross was bound for Colón at last and the long delayed reunion with his family. The baby was four months old now. As Ross entered his home, the baby stared with big brown eyes at this strange man as he kissed her mother.

Chapter 15
Renegade Preacher

Everything seemed to come apart at once for Charles Rogers. The even tenor of his life was threatened by some disruptive changes that made him feel uncomfortable, frightened even. He lived frugally and well in a small house with his wife, Henrietta, and eight children. For years he had worked steadily for the United Fruit Company, loading bananas down at the dock as many West Indians did. He was now a foreman, and he liked this position and the little increase in his paycheck. A steady, diligent man but not a brilliant thinker, he liked the security of the job, the routine of the work, and the easy camaraderie of the men he worked with and had known since childhood. He did not like change, but changes were coming—wrenching changes in all areas of his life.

Charles was a leader in the Seventh-day Adventist church in Port Limón, Costa Rica, a member of long standing who had held many offices, and now he was head elder in the church. In this capacity he served with devotion and dignity, taking great pleasure in the well-ordered routine of the work week and the Sabbath. He believed in his heart that this routine would continue throughout all eternity, for he had read in his Bible, "The new heavens and the new earth, which I will make, shall remain. . . . And it shall come to pass, that from one new moon to another, and from one sabbath to another, shall all flesh come to worship before me, saith the LORD" (Isaiah 66:22, 23).

Changes began in the government first of all. In recent years politics in Costa Rica had been unusually strong and stable, but now there were mur-

murings and unrest throughout Central America. People were agitated, and men were talking and growing restless. All of this unease meant nothing to Charles until it reached down to his job, and then it began to take on disquieting proportions. Workers were dissatisfied with the United Fruit Company, and one day there was talk of a strike. The men at the job were lining up on two sides, and the old easy fellowship was spoiled.

Charles could have let this disruption take its course and ride it out if it hadn't been for the trouble at the church. It began one Sabbath morning when a visitor came and introduced himself as Elder Shepherd. The Port Limón church, one of the most stable and reliable churches in the conference, was temporarily without a pastor. When Elder Shepherd hinted broadly that he would be glad to preach that morning, Charles was happy to hand the role over because he was very humble about his own speaking abilities. The visiting pastor was an imposing man, tall, powerfully built, immaculately dressed, and a speaker whose eloquent delivery had the "Amens" echoing from all corners. Henrietta Rogers asked him home for dinner, and he charmed the whole family.

After he left she said to Charles, "What a lovely man. Wonderful sermon this morning. I hope he can stay around here for a while, don't you?"

Charles was looking thoughtful as he replied, "I don't know. He is a good speaker, but there is something . . . something that just doesn't set right."

"Why, Charles, how can you say a thing like that! Everybody just loved him." Henrietta's eyes were snapping as she defended the visitor. "Just what was it that you didn't like?"

"I don't know, but I have learned to go by my feelings, and I have a feeling about this man," he said. Shaking his head, and not wanting to argue about it, he added, "We'll just have to wait and see."

They didn't have to wait long. The next Sabbath Elder Shepherd was there again, and when he entered the pulpit this time, he gave them his real message. He started out slowly by getting them into one accord. They were all brothers, they were all black brothers, and then he began to shoot the poisons of racial hatred into the brotherly love of his sermon. His psychology was so clever that when Charles looked around he saw to his dismay that heads were nodding and the "Amens" resounded. This time Henrietta didn't ask the pastor to dinner, but they saw him leave with the head deacon. When they were alone Henrietta said, "I see what you mean, Charles. It looks as if we may have trouble on our hands."

That week Elder Shepherd visited the parishioners, marshalling the forces to his way of thinking, and his sermon the next Sabbath was even more devastating. Charles looked down at the congregation from where he sat behind the speaker and was shocked to see that once more the visiting pastor held them in the palm of his hand as he outlined his proposal. He opened his sermon, cleverly woven around brotherly love and unity, with the words of Psalm 133:1: "Behold, how good and how pleasant it is for brethren to dwell together in unity!" His rich voice rolled the words out and hypnotized the congregation. After his introduction, he launched into his real message and began by assuring them that the church in nearby Siquirres was behind him one hundred percent. When he presented his plan, Charles and Henrietta exchanged looks of horror, as did several others, but fully a third of the members seemed to be in agreement with him. He proposed complete disassociation with the General Conference, and he led them to believe that all church property rightfully belonged to the local members and not to the Seventh-day Adventist Church. When all was said and done, Elder Shepherd had set himself up as a dictator with a takeover of the church property. He convinced the people that because they had built the churches and schools, they had the rightful title to this property and they could sue for ownership.

Elder Shepherd concluded a masterful and convincing sermon using Jeremiah 1:18: "For, behold, I have made thee this day a defenced city, and an iron pillar, and brasen walls against the whole land, against the kings of Judah, against the princes thereof, against the priests thereof, and against the people of the land." As he orated, he raised his right arm with clenched fist every time he came to the word *against,* and with such theatrics managed to inflame the congregation. They were the "defenced city," and they were against the rulers and the kings and the princes.

Charles felt the last vestige of peace and order in his world crumbling beneath him. He tried to talk with the church brothers and sisters, one to one and as a group. While two-thirds of the membership was still loyal to the church, the remaining third were aflame with this new movement. When he saw he could do nothing to stem the tide, Charles sent word to Elder Trummer asking for help right away, as this was getting out of hand.

When Elder Trummer received the letter from Charles Rogers, he called Ross into his office. "Here is a problem you have probably never encountered before," he said, pushing the letter across his desk. "Read this."

Ross shook his head as he read the letter and then exclaimed, "I can't believe this! A dictator, a revolution in the church! Where did this fellow come from?"

"He was a pastor in Jamaica and was defrocked a few years ago for bad conduct, but I have not heard of his activities since then—until now."

"How did he get a good stable church like Port Limón in such an uproar?" Ross wanted to know. "It has always been one of our most loyal churches."

"Yes," Elder Trummer replied, "that is a surprise, but don't underestimate this man's abilities. He is a gifted speaker and a brilliant thinker, and has an attractive personality. But we are told that some of the brightest lights will go out," he sighed, looking sadly at the letter.

"What are we going to do to stop this?" Ross asked. "Not only is it an awkward and embarrassing situation, but according to Brother Rogers, dangerous too. He says Elder Shepherd has threatened the life of anyone who interferes."

"I know, Ross, and I hate to ask anyone to go there, but the problem has to be dealt with, and I think you can handle it. Will you go?"

"Of course, I will go if that is your desire. But do you really want me to do this? There are other men in the conference older and more qualified." Ross was thirty-two years old at this time, and taking on this awesome responsibility was somewhat frightening to him. "This is such a complicated situation," he continued, "and there is so much riding on the outcome, I . . . I—"

"I wouldn't send you if I didn't think you could deal with it. You have had a lot of experience working with these people." Elder Trummer spoke thoughtfully. "I have been impressed by your diplomacy and courage. Put your trust in the Lord. I am convinced you are the man for the job. The conference brethren and I will be praying for you."

Ross left the president's office with the feeling that disaster was hanging over him. Feeling more helpless than he had that lonely, ominous night at Gandoca, he prayed late into the night and then fell into a restless sleep. Without giving Gertrude the details of his mission, he left early the next morning, bidding her and the baby goodbye, and prayerfully began his journey to Port Limón.

When he reached Port Limón, he went to the home of Charles Rogers. The two men and a few of the faithful in the church prayed and discussed the revolution. Charles was discouraged and depressed. Not only was the country itself in general confusion, for it looked as if the revolutionary forces were going to gain control, but the United Fruit Company workers were on strike, and now the church was falling apart. All of the tidy compartments of his life's pattern were breaking down, and it was almost more than he could bear. There seemed to be no solution, and the rift that could deal a death blow to the church and the work in that area was widening.

Then one day during a session of prayer the obvious solution struck Ross. He arose from his knees smiling and said, "Brothers, I think the answer to the problem has come to me. First of all, we must get legal basis for controlling the church building and establishing our legal rights."

"That's right," said Charles, "but how do we do this?"

"We will go to every dissident with two members as witnesses and ask them this question, 'Do you wish to separate from the General Conference of Washington, D.C.?' "

"How is that going to help us?" asked one of the deacons with a puzzled frown.

Ross was beginning to grow excited as the plan took shape. "Apparently these people are not aware that the deed to the church is held by the General Conference. If they separate from the General Conference, they will have no right to the property." He turned toward the group of men with a look of triumph now that the solution seemed within reach.

Leaping to his feet Charles exclaimed, "Elder, I think you have the answer. Let's put it into action."

The elders visited and polled all of the maverick members and then called a business meeting. The loyal members voted to accept the resignation from the church of those who wished to separate from the General Conference, and since they were then declared nonmembers, the agitators no longer had any legal rights to the church building. Those who had been misled were confounded by this strategy and ended their active involvement, but the renegade preacher was enraged. From his headquarters in the interior he swore vengeance. He sent word that if Ross or anyone from the General Conference came into the interior, he would not get out alive.

Since the insurrectionists were in almost complete control at the Siquirres church, Ross knew that he had to go there next to quash the rebellion, so he set out in spite of the fears that some in Port Limón felt for his safety. When he got to Siquirres, he found that the church elder and a few others were still loyal. The next day being Sabbath, Ross thought he should take complete charge of the Sabbath School and church service, as the presence of one of the faithful ones might infuriate the malcontents into violence.

It was truly a divided church that morning as Ross walked alone up to the rostrum and opened the meeting. All of the heretics were there, regarding him with obvious hate. About a dozen of the old guard sat in the front seats. It was an unlovely atmosphere in which to be breaking the bread of life, but he had to push on with the service. They sang the old songs with no feeling of love or fellowship. Sullen eyes were focused on the preacher, but all went quietly until Ross called for the offering. At that point one of the rebels sprang to his feet and shouted, "Not one cent of our money will go to the General Conference." He then took up an offering among his cohorts while one of the deacons passed a basket to the faithful few in the front rows.

Ross taught the Sabbath School lesson and then preached a sermon on God's love and grace, never once referring to the trouble that hung in the air like a cloud. After the service as he stood at the door, a man detached himself from the group and walked up to Ross, ordering menacingly, "Get off these premises at once! We don't want your kind here on our property."

"I'm sorry," Ross replied, "but this property belongs to the General Conference, and I intend to remain right here and protect it!"

"You'll be sorry, you meddling young upstart!" exclaimed the insurgent brother, shaking his fist as he led his followers away from the church. Ross and the elder were left alone wondering what their next move should be.

They went into the church to discuss the matter and pray about it. After prayer Ross said, "I'm impressed that I should stay here in the church in case they come back and take over the property after we leave." The two men fixed up a classroom as temporary quarters and also barricaded the building. Satisfied they had done all they could, Ross insisted the elder should go home to his family.

"I hate to leave you," he said. "We'll bring you something to eat later, and we will all be praying for you."

Ross remained in the building all night and the next day, but on Sunday afternoon he realized suddenly that he had neglected one precaution, for he had not made provision for any legal protection. He knew he could not remain alone indefinitely, and if the outlaws came to force possession he would have no choice but to submit to their demands and lose the church. He would have to go to San José to a lawyer whom the conference had employed for making up legal documents in the past.

That evening when his elder friend brought his supper, Ross asked, "Do you remember the name of that lawyer in San José from whom the conference gets legal advice?"

"Yes, Elder, I know him."

"Will you go with me tomorrow to see him?"

"Sure, but what can he do?"

"We must get a legal document of church ownership preventing the opposition from taking over. We can slip away early in the morning before anyone is up, and they will think I'm still here."

Early Monday morning the two men boarded the train for San José, found the lawyer, and outlined their plight. He was very helpful, insisting upon going back with them with authorization to take control of the building. They arrived in Siquirres on Wednesday at noon, hoping they had not been missed. The three men walked the few blocks from the train station to the church, and as they turned the corner they were dumbfounded by what they saw. Stopping, they stood there looking at each other in consternation and then at the site of the church, for it was gone! They were staring at a vacant lot. There was nothing there. Not even a stick of wood.

"They've torn the church down," Ross gasped hoarsely. "I can't believe it. What a cowardly thing to do. They will stop at nothing!"

"Oh, no," the local elder moaned, close to shock at the sight. "Our little church where we used to meet as brothers destroyed—gone."

"Mr. Sype, do you have the power of attorney for the conference?" the lawyer asked.

"No, but I can cable Colón to send us someone," Ross replied.

A few days later the conference treasurer arrived and drew up legal documents so that anyone else who tried to disturb the church property would find himself in prison. Having completed these legal safeguards, the treasurer and the attorney left, and Ross returned to Port Limón, making sure things were under control there before returning home.

In Port Limón the trouble had died down as suddenly as it began. One by one and two by two the wanderers came back, apologizing for the trouble. They were at a loss to understand how they could have been so hoodwinked by Elder Shepherd. In a few weeks all was again in harmony in that church. The renegade preacher disappeared, taking his ideas with him.

Not long after, the elder at Siquirres wrote to the conference office saying that the iconoclasts had repented and wished to be forgiven. They were willing to do anything in their power to make amends, so the conference pardoned them and accepted them back into the church.

A couple of months later, Ross received a letter from the elder at Siquirres. As proof of their remorse, the repentant members who had torn down the old church had now built another to take its place. "For we can do nothing against the truth, but for the truth" (2 Corinthians 13:8), Ross mused. "Those words mean more to me than ever before." Once again he saw how after a disaster or, in this case, a human catastrophe, after the calamity was over, the work went forward with greater vigor than before.

Chapter 16
Georgana

After several increasingly serious attacks of tropical malaria, Ross realized he would have to go to a northern climate before it became too late. The doctor had already warned him that another bout might run into the dreaded black water fever, so after consulting with Elder Pohle, the new president, he decided he should take a leave of absence. That fall he set off for the Autumn Council at Milwaukee, Wisconsin, so he could determine what course to take. Gertrude and Minita Belle went on ahead to visit with relatives in the United States, and Ross boarded a steamer later for New York by way of Haiti.

This was his second visit to Haiti, at that time considered the most primitive and backward land in the Western hemisphere. When Ross made his first visit, the officials had just punished one of the last cases of cannibalism. One of the most unusual pictures Ross had in his collection was of those cannibals in the act of feasting upon the flesh of a native Christian, which he had gotten from an Adventist missionary. He had been with the American soldiers during World War I who tracked down and caught the cannibals. He showed the picture a few times in slide-illustrated lectures of the Caribbean, but people were so disgusted and horrified that he put it away and subsequently lost it.

Ross traveled on to New York and caught a train bound for Milwaukee. When his friend, Elder A. R. Ogden, president of the Washington Conference, learned that Ross was planning to locate in a field with a suitable climate for his health, he came to the council meetings declaring that his state was an ideal place to recover from malaria, and he had a church in need of a pastor. So Ross was invited to serve as pastor of the Bellingham, Washington, church.

He was especially happy to go to Washington because his mother was at that time home missionary secretary of the Washington Conference, and his sister, Anna, and her family were living across Puget Sound from Seattle. Several other relatives lived near Seattle, so, happy to be among relatives and friends, the family moved to Bellingham and set up housekeeping.

They bought a little home on the edge of the city on a couple acres of land and enjoyed living and working in the cool climate, where all symptoms of malaria vanished. Ross felt fit and healthy, and in a northern climate, Gertrude felt her old vigor return. The following December their second baby was born, a little girl whom they named Georgana. The sisters were not at all alike, for while Minita was quiet and serious, Georgana was happy-go-lucky and very independent. Minita liked to dress up her little sister and take her for a ride in the baby carriage, but Georgana would tear her hat from her head and pull off her shoes and throw them out onto the sidewalk. Then she would laugh while Minita picked them up and patiently put them back on her.

No one ever forgot the sunny morning when Georgana, a busy toddler by then, ran away. Engrossed in playing in the backyard, Minita Belle didn't miss her at first, but when she looked up from making mud pies, Georgana was nowhere in sight. She ran into the house, thinking the little girl had gone in for a drink, but she was not there. When she told her mother, Gertrude became alarmed and the two of them ran through the house and out into the yard calling Georgana's name and stopping to listen for a reply. But they heard nothing. Then Minita Belle had an inspiration. "Let's look in the park," she said, close to tears. "She likes those swings." So they hurried breathlessly over to the park and found the lost little girl on the swing. They could hear the squawk of the swing and found her, with shrill little voice singing, head thrown back, and the breeze catching her hair.

Gertrude wanted to spank her for running away, but seeing the happy little face, she could only snatch her up in her arms and say, "You must not go to the park alone."

Minita Belle hugged her sister, kissed her and fussed over her and, holding the dimpled little hand tightly all the way home, scolded, "Georgana, you must never run away from me again."

The long happy days in Washington when the sisters played together passed by like a dream. One day Minita Belle decided to make a teeter-totter with an old board and a chunk of wood. She helped fat little Georgana sit on one end, and she herself got on the other, and they went up and down singing at the top of their voices, "Teeter-totter, bread and water, wash your face in dish water." The words half remembered from an old nursery rhyme and half made up went on and on, and at each fresh line there were gales of laughter. Suddenly Minita thought she would get her dolly to enjoy the ride, and when Georgana was up in the air, Minita jumped off. The little girl came down with a resounding bump and the fall knocked the wind out of her. She lay gasping for air and bleeding from a cut just above her eye. Thinking her sister was dying, Minita ran screaming into the house to get her mother. Gertrude ran out to pick up the sobbing child while a frightened Minita tried to offer comfort.

One day in Bellingham while the girls were playing downstairs, a fire broke out in the kitchen. Minita Belle saw the smoke and, taking her sister by the hand, she called to her mother, who was upstairs. The cry of "fire" has strange effects upon people, and under the terror of that word, they will do unreasonable things. Gertrude, alone with the two children, felt panic. She ran down the stairs, almost falling, and grabbed the girls. Not knowing what else to do with them, she put them in the car parked out front of the house. She returned then and went to the phone. When the operator said, "Number please," Gertrude screamed, "Fire!" and hung up the receiver, giving no name or address. She then rushed to her closet and put a few hats in a bag and ran out to the car with them. Returning to the house, she frantically began gathering up knick-knacks in the living room. Fortunately, just then Ross's brother-in-law and his two boys appeared at the door, saw the smoke, hurried outside, grabbed the water hose, and put the fire out.

Suddenly remembering the little girls out in the car, Gertrude ran to get them, but somehow in the scuffle they had released the brake. She arrived just as the car started rolling down the hill. She could hear their voices, shrill with fright, screaming, "Mother, Mother," and see the two wide-eyed faces staring out the back window. The boys who had put the fire out again came to the rescue. One of them sprinted down the hill, leaped into the car, and brought it to a stop.

After two years in Bellingham, Ross was elected a delegate to the General Conference session in Milwaukee. He boarded the train with Gertrude and the children, who rode as far as South Dakota, where they left him to go on to Iowa and spend the time with her family while Ross was at the conference meetings. He bade them goodbye at the depot, kissing each one and holding them close for a moment.

The days in Iowa with family and friends passed pleasantly for Gertrude and the girls. The girls became acquainted with cousins whom they had known only through letters. They had a happy and harmonious time for the most part except for a few scraps. Georgana was a spunky little girl, and when Cousin Hugh teased her, her first thought was to run for help. She started up the basement steps saying, "I go tell my mother," but when she got halfway up she stopped, turned around, and said in a determined voice, "No, I take care of you myself." She returned and began pummeling the now startled Hugh.

When they went to the Hunt picnic, an annual family reunion, Gertrude and her girls met a host of cousins, once, twice, three times removed, and aunts and uncles without number. Soon getting acquainted with the other little girls, they played house under the trees with pinecones and sticks and watched the men and boys play an intense game of softball with a lot of yelling that did not quite make sense to them. When the tables were spread under the trees with an astonishing array of food, they found out what wonderful cooks and hearty eaters and great storytellers the Hunts were. Later there was ice cream dipped out of a huge container by young men with sleeves rolled up. Since it was Minita's fifth birthday, a cake had been made especially for her, complete with candles, and everybody sang "Happy birthday to you."

In the meantime, Ross arrived at the great building in Milwaukee where the conference was held. Here he renewed old friendships. Among the first was the president of the Antillean Union Conference in the Inter-American Division, who at once said, "Well, how is the malaria?"

"I have been free from any symptoms since living in Washington—feel good—great, in fact," Ross answered.

"Don't forget you are only in the States for a leave of absence. We are expecting you back in Inter-America when the doctors decide you are well." He moved off, saying, "We will be looking for you."

In a few days the call came for Ross to return to the Inter-American Division as home missionary secretary of the Jamaica Conference. He sent word to Gertrude and then proceeded to his new field immediately. He located a nice house with a yard for the children to play in and a number of fruit trees—mango, ackie, banana, avocado, and breadfruit. Fixing up the house, along with his work, kept him busy as he waited for his family to join him.

There was nothing special about one particular day as Ross walked to town in the morning coolness to get the mail. Later he planned to go out to visit some of the isolated members on the island. The sun shone out of a clear sky, and the air was pleasant before the sun began to bear down. Seeing the Harvest Festival in full swing, he wandered around the streets until he spied some little girls' dresses. Thinking of his own two darlings about to arrive from the United States, he picked out two in pastel colors, blue for Minita Belle and pink for Georgana.

Arriving home a little later, he sat down to read the mail. The quiet was broken by a knock on the door, where a boy stood holding out a cablegram. Ross tore it open, and he saw that it was from Gertrude. It told him in the terse, cold way of cablegrams that Georgana was dead and a letter would follow. He felt faint and would have fallen if the messenger had not helped him to a chair. Staring at the thing in his hands, he did not drink the water the boy brought, nor did he hear him ask if he should call someone.

Somehow the day went by, and still Ross sat alone. No one called from the office, as it was assumed he was out in the field. The cold he had been nursing for a week grew worse, and before evening he was having difficulty breathing. It was then that chills and fever began and he knew he was having a malaria attack. This insidious disease strikes like a coward at a weakness in the body. Lying dormant for a while, it will erupt when the physical forces are low.

Ross made his way to bed and lay there fighting the pain and nausea that wracked him. In his semidelirious state the events of the past floated in and out of his mind.

As he tossed restlessly on his bed, it seemed as if each breath would be his last. Alone in his grief, he longed for the comforting presence of his wife. Death seemed to be very near to him, and desolation swept over him. The cold words of the cablegram leaped out at him, saying only "Georgana is dead. Letter follows." It left him with many unanswered questions. His eyes wandered over to the little dress he had bought for her, and sobs shook him. Was he going to die also? He remembered his father's death the year before and their last conversation.

"Ross, I feel I'm going to die soon."

"Are you afraid to die, father?"

"No, son, I've worked out the sin problem. When the Lord calls me, I'm ready."

Ross pondered the peaceful way his father had faced death. He seemed reconciled to the inevitable as if he were closing a beloved book. But as for himself, Ross felt some great void of broken dreams, unfulfilled plans, and the final blow, the death of his child. The tormented thought pressed down upon him—was it all going to end here? When the dreaded wave of sickness swept over him and left him gasping for breath, he cried out for Gertrude but realized she was thousands of miles away. Death seemed to sit on the edge of the bed.

Suddenly a feeling of great relief filled his soul, and he slept sweetly with no disturbing dreams and awoke the next morning refreshed. He felt almost normal and able to face the tasks of the day. The first thing he had to do was send a cablegram to Gertrude. Tears blinded him as he formed the words to acknowledge Georgana's death. He wired: "Sorrow intense. We shall feel loss keenly but must put trust in God. Ross."

A few days later he received a letter from his mother. She wrote: "Son, were you in trouble the night of October 4? I awoke in the night with a premonition about you. I spent the rest of the night on my knees agonizing with God to give you strength to bear your trial and to heal you of any physical impairment." As he read those words he marveled at the power of prayer. The prayer of a godly mother thousands of miles away was answered that night when her son faced his darkest hour.

Back in Iowa, Gertrude was crushed with her loss as the vacation, idyllic in all aspects before, had turned to grief. As September drew to a close she had been enjoying the enchantment of watching summer turn to fall. The sun was hot at midday, but the nights were cool, and each night it grew a little colder until that night of first frost when there was a light skim of ice on the water pails in the morning. The first day of October they were packing to go to Jamaica and saying goodbye to old friends and family.

The morning of October 3, Georgana was listless, became feverish, and rapidly grew worse. She had the dreaded "summer complaint" that took the lives of so many children in that day. She was taken to the hospital, but dehydration, typical of dysentery in those days before IVs had come into use, became critical, and they had to watch in anguish as the tiny body wasted away. Gertrude felt completely alone without Ross for comfort and support, although she did have family and friends who grieved with her. Minita Belle sat in her lap and tried to console her mother, gently patting her arm and telling her not to cry.

The following article, printed in the union conference paper of that time, tells the story.

Little Georgana Sype, two years old and daughter of Elder and Mrs. R. J. Sype, was laid to rest in the Nevada cemetery, Wednesday afternoon, Oct. 6, and while the father, who had been waiting for his family to come, had his grief to bear over in the Island of Jamaica, the mother mourned alone—no, not alone, for another little daughter, Minita Belle, the grandparents, other relatives and many friends, grieved with her at the death of one dear to all.

Prayer, and everything that loving hands could do, was offered for her relief, but it seemed her restoration to health was not to be. "Sometime we'll understand" the sorrows that come to us here; until then we must trust the Father above to work out every trial according to his will.

The deep sympathy of all was attested in many ways; beautiful flowers covered the little white casket, borne by four young girls; a ladies' quartette sang of faith and trust, and Doctor Morse spoke words of comfort and hope. He was assisted in the service by Elders Jays and Hicks. The church was filled and an unusually long procession followed to the cemetery, where every effort had been made to relieve the place of its most distressing features. Only the little casket, surrounded by green grass and flowers, is the picture left in memory.

Life's broken thread must be taken up again by those who are left, but it will be with a deeper longing for the day when the graves will be opened and our loved ones come from the land of the enemy.

—Mrs. Flora V. Dorcas

Mrs. Dorcas, Sabbath School secretary of the Iowa Conference, sent this personal message to the grieving mother:

Like the beautiful rosebuds dainty and sweet
    Sent you in love today,
Dear little Georgana came to your home,
    To brighten and cheer always;
The home will be lonely without her,
    But the Father above who knows,
Will send her again to her "mother's arms,"
    United forever you'll be—
Where no sorrow can come, no fears dismay,
    But cloudless sky and unending day—
Till then we must watch and wait.

Shortly after the funeral, Gertrude and Minita Belle sailed from New York. As the ship pulled up to the wharf in Kingston, Jamaica, Ross was waiting on the dock for them. Minita Belle ran to be swept into her father's arms. When he embraced Gertrude they wept together, remembering the dear one left behind in Iowa.

They thought often of the child who would remain in their memories always a little girl, never growing up into womanhood. But picking up the pieces of their life, they threw themselves into the work in Jamaica.

The following year Gertrude was expecting a baby. A Jewish family, Mike and Marion Golden, lived across the way, and Marion was also going to have a baby, her first. Mike was frequently gone on business, and, left alone, Marion, who was small, dark, and vibrant, became one of Gertrude's good friends.

Minita Belle missed Georgana more than anyone knew, and she hoped fervently for another sister. Since they had come to Jamaica she had created an imaginary playmate that she called "Little Sister." She became so real to Minita that she played dolls and house with her and took her for walks. She talked often about the new baby, always assuming that it would be a girl. One day Gertrude said, "But, Minita, it may be a boy."

Minita was sobered by this thought and sat very still thinking about it. When the solution came to her it was so simple, so wonderful, she was elated.

She thought about the fact that Mrs. Golden was going to have a baby too, and surely one of the babies would be a girl. If her mother had a boy and Mrs. Golden had a girl, they would just trade.

One day Minita slipped over to the neighbors and went in and stood very quietly just inside the door. Her big brown eyes were serious as she said, "Mrs. Golden, when the baby comes, do you want a boy or a girl?"

Marion smiled, thinking it was just a simple, childish question and replied, "I don't care which it is—just so it is a nice, healthy baby. I guess Mr. Golden would rather have a boy, but I will be happy with a boy or a girl."

Minita's expression grew more intense as she walked across the room and said, "I hope ours is a girl. I want a little sister again—a real little sister." Her voice took on a conspiratorial tone as she continued, "If our baby is a boy and yours is a girl, will you trade?"

She was so grave that Mrs. Golden didn't dare laugh, so she gathered the little schemer in her arms and said, "I am sure we will both get just the baby we want."

In a few weeks Mrs. Golden did have a baby girl, and Minita felt a surge of relief. A girl—so even if her mother had a boy, surely they could trade. She went over often to look at the tiny baby girl and the question haunted her, sleeping and waking—would they have a lovely baby girl or a boy?

She didn't have long to wait, for soon after, Gertrude went into labor. The doctor and nurse came, and Ross took Minita over to Mrs. Golden's, where she colored in a book, played with toys, and looked at the baby. She ran to the window often to look toward her home across the street.

At last Ross came to take her home. She greeted him with excited little squeals and asked while jumping up and down, "Is she here? Is she here? Is my baby sister here?"

"Yes, the baby is here," Ross replied with a smile, "but it isn't a sister, it's a little brother."

Minita turned a stricken face to Ross and then to Mrs. Golden. "A brother, a brother," she sobbed. "I wanted a sister."

"Now, now," Ross consoled, "come home and see how nice he is," and taking the dejected little girl by the hand, he bade Mrs. Golden goodbye and started for home.

When they got inside the house, Ross cautioned Minita that she must not cry and upset Mother "because," he explained, "Mother likes that little boy," and something told her that Daddy liked him too.

Minita crept into the room where Gertrude lay in bed holding the baby. She touched the soft hair with one finger and looked for a long time at the tiny puckered face. The grasping little hand caught one of her fingers, and as he held on tightly she looked at her mother and smiled. He opened wide staring eyes and grimaced, and Minita smiled back and said, "Mother, he smiled at me and he wants to hold my hand. Little brother," she cooed, touching his soft cheek lightly. "What is his name?" she asked.

"I think we will name him after Daddy—Ross Jackson Sype, Junior."

Minita nodded her approval, and then suddenly she remembered her bargain with Mrs. Golden. With a pang she leapt up, ran to the door, and turned to tell her mother, "I have to go over to Mrs. Golden's—something important."

When Mrs. Golden opened the door to an urgent knock, she found the little girl standing there, silent and close to tears. "Why, Minita, whatever is the matter?" she asked, drawing her inside the house.

Minita looked down at her shoes and mumbled, "The baby—our baby—it's a boy."

Mrs. Golden knelt down and put her arms around the troubled little figure and said, "A little brother. How nice, and you want to keep him, don't you?"

Blinking back the tears Minita nodded. "Well, he is our baby and—"

"And you love him. Well, I love my little girl, too. I told you we would both get the baby we wanted. Have you picked out a name yet?"

Minita stood very tall as she announced, "Yes, his name is Ross Jackson Sype, Junior. He is named after my daddy."

Chapter 17
Trouble in Jamaica

Gertrude knew there would be cockroaches in Jamaica, but she was quite unprepared for the sight that met her eyes when she opened the cupboard the morning after her arrival. Roaches that seemed to her as big as mice scurried everywhere. Her screams brought Ross running to the kitchen, his face lathered with shaving cream and blood dripping from his chin where he had cut himself. "Whatever is the matter?" he exclaimed, holding a towel to his face in an attempt to staunch the blood.

She pointed a finger toward the cupboard and shouted, "Look, just look at this!"

"Look at what?" he asked in an exasperated tone. "I only see dishes. What's wrong?"

"What is wrong? I'll tell you what is wrong—cockroaches crawling all over the place, hundreds of them as big as rats! They disappear when you open the door, but they are there—hiding." She shuddered and looked imploringly at Ross and asked, "What are we going to do?"

Ross was in a hurry to get down to the office because Elder Hurdon, the president, had asked him to come in early. A domestic crisis was not helping him get off to a good start. He had warned Gertrude and reminded her now that he had written about the insects, so she should not have been totally unprepared for them.

Gertrude recalled the rather disarming letter. He had written, "About cockroaches. Yes, there are plenty of them, but it is nothing to worry about, as the lizards keep them under control. You see, they have cute little lizards that dearly love to eat the cockroaches. If you don't mind the lizards and will let them have full range of the house, they will eat every cockroach. These little lizards are rather pretty and perfectly harmless. They climb right up the wall or any place and get after any bugs to be found. Elder Hurdon has one lizard living in each bookcase and he says his books are never bothered by roaches. I see a little lizard in my room very often, and in fact, the Hurdons give them a place of honor in the house. They may be seen most any time in the parlor or in the kitchen. Not everyone agrees, of course. Mrs. Petty is so afraid of them she chases them out of the house and sets poison for the cockroaches. As far as I am concerned, I don't mind the lizards at all. In fact, they are rather interesting. They have a merry little twinkle in the eye as they go scurrying up the wall on the lookout for a roach."

"As for that letter," Gertrude said. "When I read it to my sisters in Iowa we all had a good laugh. It seemed funny then—lizards chasing cock-roaches—'pretty little things, merry twinkle in their eye.' But I don't want cockroaches, and I don't want those slinky, horrid lizards crawling around the house either."

Ross shrugged. "Very well, it's up to you, but I see nothing wrong with a few little harmless lizards," and he retreated to the bedroom to finish his dressing, leaving a disgruntled Gertrude to grapple with the cockroach quandary.

Gertrude's domestic duties in the tropics were quite different from those in the United States. Although maids were readily available, Gertrude hesitated at turning her kitchen or her children over to native help. She had a succession of domestics, but until Ivy came from Mile End, she never found one to be really satisfactory. She was very finicky about sanitation and never did "go native" in her cooking but continued to prepare food the same way she had in Iowa. While uncomfortable about many local customs, she did like to buy fruit and vegetables from vendors.

Later that same morning, Gertrude was in the kitchen kneading bread when she heard a loud, strident call from the street. It was the vendor who came along almost every morning, a tall, angular native woman yelling at the top of her voice, "Yams! Nice ripe bananas!" as she walked along bal-ancing her load of produce in a large basket on her head. Since Gertrude needed some fruit and vegetables, she went to the door, clapped her hands, and beckoned to the woman, who ambled over and deliberately took her basket off her head and placed it on the top step. Minita came to watch, fascinated by the whole process. After the purchase, the woman wound a cloth in a circle, put it up on top of her head, and lifted the basket on top of that. Then she went down the street with majestic balance, the rich voice shouting her wares.

When Ross arrived at the office that morning, he went directly to confer with Elder Hurdon over a letter he had received. "I have a letter here from Brother Williams," he said, "and he informs me they have twenty ready for baptism up in that mountain village where they have been holding meetings. He wants me to come and baptize them."

Elder Hurdon picked up the letter Ross pushed across the desk and studied it for a moment. "Twenty people!" he exclaimed. "Praise the Lord! But what about this opposition? Sounds as if the priest is out to get the pastor."

"Yes, it does. In fact, he has stirred up the mountain folk to make sure a baptism doesn't take place. They have warned the group of believers that if a minister comes up there, a mob of a thousand people will break up the service and run the preacher off the mountain."

"A pretty strong threat. Do you think you ought to take the risk? You know how dangerous mob violence can become."

"It can get ugly all right," Ross replied, "but I won't be put off by their threats. I've written to Brother Williams that if there are twenty people to be baptized, I will come if the mountain is full of devils. I am sure the Lord will protect us."

The incredible story of this missionary project up in a mountainous region in Jamaica had already reached Kingston. Members of a large, prospering church in the lowlands at the foot of the mountains had felt a burden for people in the lush valleys as well as in the village at the top of the mountains who did not know Jesus. Although there were no roads, only narrow trails, and the sole means of transportation was by foot or donkey, the church members were determined to carry the message to them.

Each Sabbath the people in this missionary-minded church brought their lunch, and after eating they began the difficult climb up the twisted paths to

the little settlement at the top of the mountain. Carrying bundles of literature on their heads, they labored up and up, some riding donkeys, others on
foot, and many barefoot. The procession wound single file along the tortuous
footpath. Children skipped along; young people maneuvered to walk with
their heart's desire; and older folks plodded on using knobby sticks to help
them over the rough way.

The village clung to the mountain seemingly in defiance of gravity. Beaten
paths led the way between houses; chickens and dogs roamed everywhere.
Children played in the shade and men and women lounged by the buildings.
Upon arriving, the procession would go to the Chinese shop, the gathering
place for the rural villagers. Under a nearby tree they would start singing.
Although the Chinese who owned the shops didn't show much interest in the
meetings, they allowed the villagers to meet there.

Attracted by the singing, the loafers in the streets edged closer, women
wandered over from their houses, and men walked in from the little gar-
dens where they had been tending their crops. Children crowded in close
and, prompted by the visiting children, soon joined in the singing. After
the song service one of the missionaries gave a short Bible study. The
missionaries came here faithfully week after week and month after month
till the mountain people began to look forward to the meetings. Hearts
were touched and many accepted the message. Brother Williams then
sent the letter to Kingston announcing that twenty people were ready for
baptism.

Ross was determined to go up the mountain to baptize these converts. As
he walked home to get ready for the trip he met Bert, a young man from his
church. He told Bert where he was going and added, "I don't look forward to
the walk up that mountain. Do you know where I can get a donkey? Besides
the long steep climb, there are the supplies and gear I have to take with
me."

By this time they had reached Ross's house, and seeing the roadster parked
outside, Bert said, "Why don't you drive up?" Ross became interested at once
and asked, "Do you think the old Dodge could make it up that rough
trail?"

Although his knowledge of cars was next to nothing, Bert walked around
the battered vehicle, kicked each tire expertly, patted it on the hood, and

said, "I think so. There is one trail that is wider than the others. I tell you what, if I go along and show you that trail, I think she can make it."

Looking back later, Ross wondered why he had put so much stock in the advice of a young man untrained in mechanics, but at the time it seemed like a good idea, and it appealed to his daring-do nature. Unfortunately, Gertrude was not home to stop the mad scheme. Within the hour the two men had packed what they needed and were on their way. They drove to the foot of the mountain and began the ascent, steep from the very beginning. Ross had the car in low gear, but the farther they went up the continuous steep climb on what was a mere donkey path, the more foolhardy the venture seemed. Once started, they had to go ahead, for there was no place to turn a car around.

Ross hung on to the steering wheel with grim determination, expecting at any moment to do some irreparable damage to the car or to them. Bert, on the other hand, was aglow with excitement as Ross jockeyed between rocks, over fallen branches, and through tangled vines, with brush slapping the fenders on either side as they followed the narrow path. Although his tall thin body was whipped about without mercy, he felt elated, and above the grinding of the engine he shouted, "Ain't this something? A car has never been up here before. This will be a first. Those folks up there will really be surprised to see us drive in," and he grinned at the heady thought.

"They won't be as surprised as I will," Ross muttered. Just then they heard an ominous hissing from the radiator, and a plume of steam escaped from the hood. The smell of hot metal hung in the air, and Ross pressed on the brake, bringing the car to a shuddering halt. Steam poured from the car as it sat there in the heat with its nose pointed up.

"What happened, Elder Sype?" Bert asked. "Why are we stopping? We were just getting going." His education in the baffling field of mechanics was about to begin.

"The water has boiled out of the radiator. We'll have to let it cool off and find some water before we can go on," Ross explained. He took a can out of the car that he carried for emergencies, and after finding a spring of water, Ross filled the radiator, and they were able to resume the journey. The trail grew even steeper, and Ross would have gladly traded the car for a strong little donkey. More than once he thought, *What was I thinking of? What will Gertrude say?*

At long last they reached the top, only to find more trouble waiting. The welcome committee was composed of a sizeable mob looking less than welcoming. The village priest and his followers had been listening for some time to the car grinding away at the ascent. A great roar greeted Ross and Bert as they rolled past the rabble and headed for the house of the leader of the group that was to be baptized. Ignoring the threats as best as they could, they parked outside and ducked into the house when the door was opened by a worried and concerned Brother Banks. He pulled the men inside and quickly shut the door. His frightened wife and the three children cowered in the next room, peeking out from time to time. Brother Banks's face twitched and he rubbed his hands together. "I am sorry about this," he said, "but the village priest is upset about the new religion."

"Upset! Well, I'd really hate to meet up with them when they are angry," Ross said.

Bert had stopped talking and all traces of his cocksure grin had vanished. Ross looked from one frightened face to another and felt considerable fear himself, but he knew he would have to confront the mob sooner or later. There was no way out. He prayed for wisdom and strength, and stepped to the door saying, "I will have to go out there." Mrs. Banks gave a little gasp, and Mr. Banks held out a hand as if to deter him, but he brushed past, opened the door, and stepped out.

The sun was just going down, casting a reddish glow over the sea of angry faces before him as his eyes swept back and forth looking for the leader. One individual stood out, a hulking man positioned slightly in front, leading the chants. He was huge, a veritable Goliath, wearing a ragged shirt that showed his well-muscled torso. His bullet-shaped head was covered with short cropped hair, and his mouth was drawn back in an intimidating snarl. Ross knew he did not dare to hesitate nor draw back; so he walked up to him with a smile and reached out to shake hands, saying disarmingly, "Good evening, friend." Caught off guard, the burly leader found himself shaking hands with the enemy, and his unfriendly expression changed to bewilderment and chagrin as he realized the significance of the act, for in Jamaica, to shake hands means friendship.

"What a pleasure to meet you and your friends and to visit your beautiful village. What magnificent scenery," Ross went on, smiling and waving his hand toward the peaks and valleys around them.

"Yes suh. Thank you," the mob leader found himself saying while his friends stood with mouths open, watching him consort with the very one he was going to run off the mountain. Ross then walked around shaking hands and speaking to some of the others in the group.

The mob was baffled by this turn of events and even more so when he said, "Now, friends, I hope to see you again while I am here. We're having a baptism down by the river Sunday morning. Hope you can come."

"We'll be there, boss," they assured him as they drifted away in different directions. He didn't doubt that they would be there, for they had already assured him there would be a thousand people at the riverside to break up the baptism.

The next day was Sabbath, and the little group worshiped together in their new thatched-roof chapel. The church was filled with the believers from the village and friends from the lowland church. The Sabbath drew to a close with no further trouble, and the car stood out in the street without being bothered all weekend.

It was an old custom in Jamaica to hold baptisms on Sunday morning, so the next morning a group of the faithful wound its way down the steep trail. As they rounded the last curve and the river came in view, what a sight greeted them! Up and down the stream on each side people were sitting, standing, or milling around, hundreds of people, easily the thousand they had promised. When they came in sight of the mob, the troublemakers began chanting and yelling. The valley echoed with their shouts, and the believers stopped in their tracks, afraid to go on. Turning to Ross they said, "Elder, what can we do? They will kill us."

"Stay here," Ross replied, "and pray. I am going down to look for the best place for the baptism."

As he neared the riverbank he spotted the big man who had led the mob on Friday night. Walking up to the troublemaker he said warmly, "Well, here is my friend. Hello, Sam," for he had learned his name, and he shook the huge hand, all the while smiling and looking around at a thousand people ready to do him harm. "I am so happy you can be with us this morning," he went on. "Say, you seem to have unusual influence over these people. I wonder if I could count on you to help me during the service." A pleased smile crossed Sam's face, and in spite of himself, he warmed to the compliment.

"The baptism is going to begin in a few minutes," Ross continued. "Would you please keep the crowd quiet while I bring the candidates down to the water?"

Sam's head nodded agreeably. "All right, preacher."

The cluster of frightened souls waiting there didn't know what to do, but when Ross beckoned to them they made their way down the path, single file, treading warily. The young minister and the first convert stepped into the water, and at that second a tremendous shout shook the valley, drowning out the singing of the assemblage on the bank. Immediately Big Sam rose importantly from his perch on a rock, put his finger to his lips and uttered a sonorous *"Sh-h-h!"* The shouting stopped at once, and in the reigning silence the baptism proceeded in an orderly and reverent manner. The agitators began to disperse, and soon Ross was left alone on the bank of the river with the faithful little group.

After the service they crowded around, asking, "Elder, what happened? What did you do? How did you control them?"

"Weren't you all praying?" he replied. "Did you not expect the Lord to answer your prayers?"

A few weeks later Ross again traveled up the trail to visit the mountain company, but this time he rode a donkey, a sturdy, willing animal called Mose. As he was tying Mose to a post Brother Banks came rushing out to greet him. "So you decided on donkey back this time," he said, laughing.

Giving Mose a fond pat, Ross replied, "There are places for cars and places for donkeys, and that trail is more suited to a donkey. So how is the company doing? I thought I had better come up and see how things are going. Has Sam and that bunch given anymore trouble?"

"No, Elder, no trouble at all," Brother Banks answered. "And there is a family in the next valley from where the baptism was held that is very interested. They have made arrangements to hold an outdoor service at the local Chinese shop and want you to come down there."

"Wonderful," Ross replied. "Let's send a messenger telling them they can expect us tomorrow afternoon."

A tall gangly boy who lived across the street was duly sent down the valley and in a few hours came scrambling back, breathless with the exertion of the run. He clattered up to the house and, scarcely bothering to knock, burst into the room. "The folks want you to come and hold a service," he announced, "but some of Sam's gang met me on the trail coming back and they said to come ahead if you want to get your head broke. They said any preacher that comes into their valley will have to be carried out. Then they said, 'Tell him we will be waiting for him with clubs.' " The boy paused to catch his breath and added with a confident smile, "But after the way you handled them at the baptism, those threats won't mean nothing."

"This is God's business, you know," Ross replied gravely, "and He does look after His own. All the Sams on this island cannot stop God's work."

The next morning Ross and Brother Banks began their journey down the narrow, tangled path. They walked for a long time with sweat running into their eyes and insects following them, but they pressed on until at last the trail opened into a clearing, with native shops on both sides of a dirt street that threaded its way through the village. As they neared the Chinese shop they passed a vacant lot where a huge tree had fallen. Sitting along the entire length of the tree were about twenty huge, scowling men, and in each hand was a club.

Trying not to show fear, Ross paused and greeted them. "Good morning. We are having a meeting this afternoon and would like for you to come."

One of them replied through tight lips, "Oh, yes, we will be there all right." He brought his club down on a little branch, smashing it to pieces.

The two men walked on to the shop, where, at the appointed time, about fifty people came for the service. Ross stood in front and led them in singing several hymns followed by a prayer. When he opened his eyes Ross turned cold upon seeing the group of ruffians coming up the trail, marching like soldiers, still carrying their clubs. Walking with slow menacing steps, they came closer and closer until they had surrounded the preacher, cutting him off from the congregation. They leered at him with anger and hate on their faces, and one who stood directly in front made grotesque facial contortions ending in a toothless snarl.

Ross began speaking as if nothing was out of the ordinary, taking for his text 2 Peter 3:13: "Nevertheless we, according to his promise, look for new heavens and a new earth." He went on to tell them about that grand and glorious day when our precious Jesus will come and end all sickness and death, about that place where we will know only happiness and love.

At this point in his sermon he heard the toothless one whisper to the man next to him, "He's all right." This message was passed from one to the other down the line. Upon reaching the last one they laid down their clubs, folded their arms and gradually, one by one, merged with the crowd and sat down. No one moved then, but all listened with great interest to the wonderful story of Christ's coming to this earth and putting an end to the misery and poverty that was so well known in the lives of these mountain people.

At the close of the service the people greeted Ross warmly, and they begged him to return, some with tears in their eyes. From this beginning, two churches were organized in that area, one on the mountain and another in the valley.

Chapter 18
Mile End

Although Ross never again drove the Dodge up that mountain trail, he did dare to negotiate the road that wound up to a place called Mile End, and the car was able to arrive with few problems. By this time the old Dodge roadster, a serious, no-nonsense car, was a familiar sight on the roads of the island. It commanded the same kind of respect and affection you would give a horse or a dog that served well and faithfully without complaint. Scratched and dented, it was by no means a thing of beauty, and had shuddered to a stop many times seemingly done for, with steam spewing from the radiator and sides heaving with the effort. With a little rest, a little cooling off, and a little water, it was on the move again. It took the steep pitches in its own slow, ponderous time, scratching for the top, or again descending, holding back against the murderous strength of gravity.

Among the hazards Ross met on the way to Mile End were the native people who ambled along in the middle of the road, either walking or riding a mule. Ross always feared that he would run into someone, and he did have that terrifying experience one day coming down a series of switchbacks at dusk. The visibility was poor, and he was thinking of something else when a man on horseback suddenly appeared right in front of him. He fought to slow the car and avoid a collision but to no avail. There was a sickening crash. Ross jumped out of the car, fearing what he might find only to see a man standing by the side of the road and the horse nowhere in sight.

"Where is the man I hit?" Ross shouted.

"I'se him," replied the man, who smelled strongly of beer and tried to steady himself by leaning against the car.

"How did you get off that horse?" asked Ross.

"Jump, boss," the man answered, and picking up his hat from the ditch, he settled it on his head and began a rather uncertain route up the mountain on foot, leaving Ross staring incredulously at the accident victim.

Mile End was a mountain settlement five or six miles from the coast. Innocent of cars or machines of any kind, it could only be reached by the trail that led up from the main road. The loose-knit community consisted of a collection of houses scattered in the valley and on the sides of the mountain and others well up to the top, where there was a nice little church. The heart of the community was a clear bubbling stream that ran to the foot of a hill and was the center for washing, bathing, and getting water for drinking and cooking.

This colony had its origin one night in 1801, when three conscripted seamen from Scotland jumped ship from a British freighter and under cover of darkness swam to shore. They didn't know exactly where they were, but anything was better than their unwilling servitude on shipboard. They had been kidnapped in a pub in Aberdeen by the British and had been virtual slaves ever since. This much they did know—they were somewhere between the United States and Central America.

Accustomed to swimming in cold water because they had swum in the cold seas around their native Scotland as boys, the three men made their way with little difficulty to a beach, where they found a veritable paradise with food readily available and plenty of fresh water. Making their way up a rough mountain some five or six miles from the coast, they erected shelters at what they called Mile End and scouted the land for farming possibilities. The land was fertile beyond imagination, perfect for growing sugarcane in the lowlands and coffee in the highlands, so they decided to settle down and farm.

There was one obstacle to their plan. The three men, Bruce Macdonald, Robert Campbell, and William Burns, had no money, only the clothes on their backs, so they made their way down to Kingston and got jobs unloading cargo boats. They were very careful to save their money and to keep away from bars, where unscrupulous skippers were often on the lookout for men. A crack on the head with a club or a little laudanum surreptitiously poured into your ale and you would wake up on a boat far out at sea. One experience like this had made the men wary of smooth-talking strangers in bars.

They could have gotten passage home on a ship but decided that since fate had placed them here, they would try their luck. Besides, they had fallen in love with this fair land far from the cold rains of Scotland. After working for two years, the men bought tools, went back to Mile End, and began to grub out their plantation. The work was slow and backbreaking. One day Bruce Macdonald stopped and, wiping his brow, said to his friends, "Boys, we have to figure out some other way to get this work done."

Robert and Will nodded in agreement and sat down for a rest. Suddenly Will had an inspiration that electrified them all. "What we need is some slaves like those farmers around Kingston have working for them."

Robert stood up as if he were leaving right then and exclaimed, "Well, let's go get them!"

"Wait a minute, now," Bruce cautioned, "they cost a lot of money. How much do we have left after we bought all those tools?"

Will, who acted as treasurer, did a little figuring and then replied, "I think we only have enough to buy two slaves and not the best quality either."

"Two are better than none," Robert said. "Let's go down to Kingston and see what we can find."

Down at the slave market they looked longingly at strong, rugged men to work their land, but the price was prohibitive, so they bought and paid for two scrawny teenaged boys. Despite their small size and youth, they turned out to be excellent workers. With this work crew of five, they cleared land and planted crops. The next year they bought two more slaves, and the next year, with the profits from the crops, they were able to purchase six slaves, including three beautiful women whom the three Scotsmen took for their wives.

The three men soon had prospering plantations, growing families, and a comfortable way of life. Each family had a little house, and on washday the wives gathered at the river to pound out the clothes on the rocks, spread them out to dry, and gossip while the children swam and played. Many years went by before they began to hear rumors that slaves were going to be freed. News traveled slowly to the settlement on Mile End, and it wasn't until one day just before cane harvest in 1832 that an official came and knocked on Bruce Macdonald's door, informing him that the slaves had been set free.

By this time the three men owned perhaps a hundred slaves. This news was a devastating blow to their way of life. It would be impossible to keep up the plantation without the slaves, so the three men did what most of the other white landowners did at that time. They packed up what they wanted, gathered all the cash they could lay their hands on, and leaving land, slaves, wives, and children, they sailed for their homeland.

The slaves, who had done most of the work through the years, went on growing cane, harvesting coffee, and running the plantation. When Ross came to Mile End, it was populated by the descendents of those black women and Scottish men. They were a handsome people, showing traces of Scottish blood in their features even then in 1927. Many of the women were truly lovely with wonderful figures, having the erect, graceful carriage that comes from carrying loads on their heads from childhood.

Since there were no cars up on the mountain, the sound of the old Dodge grinding its way up the grade always caused a stir among the children. When they heard it leave the highway and start up the mountain they began gathering at the end of the road to welcome the minister. It took a long time for the climb up that narrow winding road full of rocks and ruts, but the children waited, full of anticipation.

One of Ross's duties was young peoples' secretary of the conference, so he organized activities for the youth. Years before the church organized Pathfinder clubs, Ross had a vision of getting young people out in nature to study God's second book. This brought a new dimension into their lives. The adults at Mile End were forced by the necessity of their subsistence farming to work long hard hours, so the children seldom knew a grown-up who could play games with them or take them on walks and study nature. Therefore, it was with great enthusiasm that they greeted the pastor.

"Elder, will you take us for a walk?" they begged one day as he parked the Dodge. Then for the first time the children of Mile End climbed to the top of the mountain. Their climb took them through magnificent scenery. Colorful birds they could not name flew up at their approach. When at last they reached the peak, the laughing and talking stopped and even the very young were silent before the splendor of the scene. The green valleys fell away behind them, and before them sparkled the sea. No one spoke for a long time until a little girl came over to Ross and, putting her hand in his, smiled up at him and said softly, "It's like being in church, huh, Elder?" "Like heaven," another spoke up. And then quite spontaneously they all began singing the hymn, "I am thinking today of that beautiful land I shall reach when the sun goeth down."

The work in Jamaica beginning in isolated mountain settlements like Mile End, as well as in lowland churches, made astonishing growth. Today it would be hard to find a place on the island where there are no Adventists, for now there is an average of one church every half mile. During a visit in 1972, Ross was gratified and jubilant at the progress he found. Workers whom he had baptized talked of the old days in those isolated areas where he held meetings and raised up churches. The president of the East Jamaica Conference, Elder White, recalled the small church he attended as a boy and told Ross it had been replaced with a large stone building. "Your name is inscribed on the foundation of that new church, Elder Sype," he said, and added that his father used to say to the boys, "Walk softly before these names. These are the men of God who founded this work."

Chapter 19
The Cayman Islands

The dark dread of leprosy has hung over humankind since antiquity. The dread is not so much for the pain, for other diseases are more painful, nor is it for the fear of death, for the ailment itself seldom kills. It is from the sure isolation from home and friends that strikes terror into hearts in places where leprosy is known. The ancient cry of "unclean" that separates the unfortunate victim of the disease from loved ones and strangers alike—it is here the horror begins.

Leprosy, called Hansen's disease for the work of a Norwegian doctor, was a dreaded disease in Bible times and has erupted in diverse places ever since, even in places far north of the tropics. The last epidemic in modern Europe occurred around the middle of the nineteenth century in pockets in Norway, Sweden, and the British Isles. No satisfactory explanation was ever found for the epidemic. But artifacts remain to remind us that once it was a reality. If you go to Bergen today you will find what was at that time a hospital for victims of Hansen's disease. The Lutheran church in Rosendal, built in the year 900, has a low window called the leper's window. Here the sufferers of Hansen's disease, not allowed to enter the church, could look in with longing eyes on the table of Christ, where the bread was broken and the goblet of wine was passed from one to another.

One man who lived on the island of Grand Cayman had to come to grips with this tragedy, and in spite of it he answered the question, "Who is my neighbor?" A colporteur from Jamaica went over to the Cayman Islands and sold David a book. David was like someone waiting for a signal, and as soon

133

as he found new light he shared it with others, organizing a little company that met every Sabbath in his home.

Then David began to notice the spots on his legs. He thought they would go away, but they did not. He didn't know until the day his hands touched live coals and he smelled burned flesh before he felt the pain that he was a leper. When he told his wife she wept, and when he told her he would now live alone, apart from her and the children, she wanted to embrace him once more, but he said, "No, you must not touch me, for I love you."

"But what about the church?" she asked.

"We will still have the church," he replied. "We must always have the church."

For several years the faithful continued meeting in David's home as they had been doing, and David preached from the next room. People came from far and near to sit outside and talk with him. He who had no hope gave hope to others. They spoke of David with a reverence that gave him a certain dignity even though he suffered from this ancient scourge that would brand him "unclean."

To sweeten under pressure is not easy. It is easy to rage, to grow bitter, to place the blame, to curse God and die, but David went on with his work. He had been a good man before, but now he became like a saint, like Father Damien. Every Sabbath the house was crowded. To hear him speak was living water—the day was better, the week went more smoothly, life itself had more meaning. He asked for a Jordan where he might be washed clean. He prayed to be healed, but he was not healed, and he worked on. The disease made slow, insidious progress, and his fingers became useless, his toes wasted away, his face began to change—to become leonine. Still, every Sabbath many people came to hear him, a voice from the next room.

The company of believers desperately needed a minister to come, for many souls were ready for baptism. One of the believers, Mrs. King, wrote to the division office begging for someone to come and help them build a small church. At last a letter lay on Ross's desk with orders to go to Grand Cayman.

After meeting with the conference officials, Ross went to Elder Sam Lawson, a Jamaican minister, and asked, "Sam, how would you like to take a trip to Grand Cayman with me?"

"I would like to very much," he replied with enthusiasm. "I've always wanted to go back there and follow up on the results of my colporteur work years ago."

So Ross told him about David and the flourishing group of believers who had been worshiping in his home for several years; of the many believers who were ready for baptism. He finished by saying, "And now these folk want to build a church. The division office wants me to decide whether a church building is feasible. They are ready to help because they are sending a signed check with me. What do you think of that?"

"Wonderful! When do we leave?"

"As soon as I can find passage for us. You know it is rather hard to find a boat of any size going to Grand Cayman. I may be able to locate a small sailing vessel in Kingston. They sometimes come from George Town to Kingston to trade. I'll send word to Mrs. King and tell her we are coming. She is the one who contacted the division in the first place."

"Mrs. King?" Elder Lawson exclaimed, "How marvelous! I distinctly remember selling her a book—*Bible Readings.* Wonderful Christian woman, a school teacher. I'll be happy to see her again."

A few weeks later, Ross and Sam Lawson engaged passage on a flimsy sailboat bound for George Town, Grand Cayman. With some apprehension Ross bid Gertrude and the children goodbye that morning, for he would be out of contact with the family for an uncertain length of time. Because there was no communication between the islands and the outside world except for little sailing vessels with an uncertain schedule, there was no way they could get in touch in case of an emergency. The islands had no wireless station, no cable facilities, nothing except the chance visit of a boat. The islanders had, in fact, more contact with America than with Jamaica, for they sailed their small boats into Mobile, Alabama, to sell turtle shells and fish and to purchase needed items such as cloth, flour, and materials for their boats.

Although the boat Ross and Sam sailed on was small and old, she was skippered by a knowledgeable captain and she fairly flew over the water, bending before the wind like a live thing. On the way to Grand Cayman something that looked like a great tall ship on the open sea suddenly loomed up in the distance. "Cayman Brac," said Elder Lawson. "Looks like a ship coming, doesn't it?" As they drew nearer they could see more closely the mighty perpendicular rock with a sharp bow like a ship. As they passed, they could see no place where a ship might land.

The watchful islanders had sighted the boat far out at sea, and when it docked at George Town, Mrs. King and Mrs. Anvil, wife of a sea captain, were there to meet it. The two ministers went to the Anvil home, and after they had rested and eaten lunch, Mrs. Anvil said, "David will want to see you. Come, we must go to his house." They sat outside his house under a tree and talked with David, who was so overcome with joy the tears ran down his disfigured face and his voice broke.

On Sabbath they attended services at David's home, and David spoke from the room of his exile while the congregation filled the rest of the house. It was so full that some had to sit on windowsills or stand outside the door. Ross was impressed not only with the number of believers present but also the keen inner joy of walking with God that each of these worshipers seemed to have experienced. It was truly an inspiring Sabbath for the two workers who had come to bring the gospel but were finding they received great blessings themselves. Seeing this enthusiasm made Ross feel safe in buying a lot for a church to be built on and paying for it with the signed check from the division office so the work could go on.

Mysteriously, like mushrooms, groups of believers seemed to spring up everywhere on these islands; a company here, a group there, or an isolated family someplace else. One group was meeting on the other side of Grand Cayman in a place called East End. This group of believers was the result of the missionary work of a young girl who had gone there from George Town.

Although the island is small, scarcely five miles wide and twenty miles long, East End in the east and George Town in the west had little contact. There was no historical connection between them, for they were descended from entirely different stock. The reason for the lack of communication was purely geographical because there were only two ways to go from one town to the other, both difficult. The best way was by boat, if you could find a boat, which was seldom, and the other way was to walk along the beach, a distance of about twenty miles.

Ross and Elder Lawson decided to go over to East End to pursue the interest there, and since they could not obtain a boat, they set out on the long walk. Walking along the beach was bad enough, with the calves of their legs knotting up from the exertion of struggling through deep sand, but when the tide came in it was worse, for they were then forced back into the jungle to pick their way through dense undergrowth, always watchful for deadly snakes, bloodsuckers, and a myriad of insects. It was a long, hot, exhausting walk, and they really did not expect to find much at the end, but they kept doggedly on, too tired to talk. They wondered if they would ever reach East End, if there was an East End, and if such a place existed, if there were any believers there or if it was just a rumor started around an evening fire.

At last they reached a settlement and people ran out, amazed to see strangers. "Is this East End?" Ross called out.

"Yes," shouted the natives. "Who are you?"

"We are Seventh-day Adventist ministers from Jamaica. We heard there are some of our faith here."

There was great excitement, with everyone talking at once. Some could not contain their elation and threw their arms around the ministers, saying they were indeed of the same faith and wanted to be baptized. These friendly people found them a place to stay and brought food and drink. They had built a little church, a thatched-covered building with no floor, but it was clean and comfortable. The men had even made benches. Ross and Sam stayed several days, holding meetings each evening. Before retiring at night they would sit outside and watch the Southern Cross making its trip across the sky over the South Pole.

One day as they were relaxing on the porch looking out over the ocean, a small sailing boat appeared on the horizon and headed for the island. They watched as it continued its course toward the beach in front of them, stopping about a half mile out beyond where the waters became shallow. Then two men boarded a hand-hewn dinghy and rowed toward shore. After beaching the dinghy, they walked up to Ross and Sam. Fixing their gaze on Ross, one of them asked, "Is your name Sype?"

"Yes," Ross replied, looking quizzically at the men, not knowing what to expect.

Mincing no words, the man informed him, "The commissioner wants you to come to his office right away. We have been sent to bring you back in our boat."

Ross was incredulous and asked, "Why does the commissioner want to see me?"

"You will have to find out when you get there. My orders are to take you to his office in George Town. You'd better get your belongings and come along."

There seemed to be no alternative, so the two men gathered up their things, said Goodbye to their host, and boarded the boat. As they sailed back to George Town under a good breeze well out from the torturous beach where they had labored step by step, Sam said with a hearty laugh, "Well, Ross, no matter what they want with us, this sure beats walking back."

When they reached the commissioner's office, a stern-faced man sitting behind a desk said, "Reverend Sype, do you know you are on this island in transgression of the law and you are subject to heavy fine and imprisonment?"

"No, sir, what have I done?" Ross exclaimed in astonishment.

"You have landed without a passport or any type of visa!" the officer said, glaring at him.

Appalled at this accusation Ross declared, "Mr. Commissioner, I investigated this matter before leaving Kingston. The immigration officer there assured me that I did not need a passport."

"But I'm telling you in no uncertain terms that you do!" stormed the commissioner. "You have broken the law and are subject to punishment!" and he pounded his desk with his fist for emphasis.

Fighting back his feelings over this injustice, Ross realized it would be futile to argue, so he said, "Your Honor, I have explained why I have no passport. If this doesn't meet with your approval and you feel I have violated the law, then I guess I will have to take whatever punishment you have for me." Shrugging, he spread his hands in a resigned manner.

To his relief, his accuser met his imploring smile with a sympathetic grin and leaning forward said, "Reverend Sype, the law does say you need a passport. The Caymans are being rough on Americans right now in retaliation for restrictions placed on them by the United States. However, the law also allows me to use my own judgment, so I am not going to prosecute you." He leaned back in his chair and regarded Ross thoughtfully as he continued. "You are in a tough spot. The immigration officer you checked with was undoubtedly unaware of a recent law that prohibits Americans from landing in the Caymans without a passport."

"Why did they pass such a law?" Ross asked.

"You probably haven't heard of the bad feeling here, but everyone in the Caymans is aware of it, and it is understandable. The Americans, you see, passed a law making it hard for Caymanians landing in the United States, so this law is aimed at getting even."

"That sure puts me in a jam," Ross exclaimed.

"You have been caught in the middle, Reverend, but our problem is to get you back to Jamaica without your landing in jail."

"What can I do?"

"There is a revolution going on in Honduras," the commissioner said thoughtfully. "Many Honduran men married Jamaican wives who renounced their Jamaican citizenship upon moving to Honduras. Now these men are trying to get their families back to their relatives and safety in Jamaica. A ship is down in the harbor right now to carry many of these refugees illegally. They plan on smuggling them into a sparsely populated area in Jamaica. I would advise you to take passage on this ship so you can avoid the authorities."

"Looks as if I don't have much choice," Ross said slowly and turned to Elder Lawson with concern. "Sam, you are in the clear since you are a native of Jamaica. You don't need to get mixed up in this."

"I'm going with you all the way," Sam vowed. "You may need me."

They took passage on the illegal ship, and from the beginning it seemed to be ill fated. No more than a few hours out to sea they fell into that bane of sailing vessels, a dead calm. Not a breeze stirred, the sails drooped, and for a day and a half they wallowed on the languid sea while a pitiless sun beat down. The refugees cried for water, and the children sought what shade they could find, their energies flagging.

Then a sudden gust of wind filled the sails and was greeted with a cry of joy that quickly turned to despair, for storm clouds loomed on the horizon and were coming toward them. The sky turned dark and the sea was whipped into waves that tossed the little craft about, threatening to break her in two. Frantic confusion broke out among the passengers as they were tossed about in the bowels of the boat. The storm seemed to be as unsparing as it was unending. Then it ended as suddenly as it began, and the waters were quiet. Although the little boat had survived, she had suffered damage, so the captain decided they should limp into nearby Cayman Brac for repairs before proceeding on their journey.

Cayman Brac, impressive as always, stood above them like the bow of a great ship. The captain knew this place well and sailed the battered little boat into port. Ross and Sam were given a cabin near the landing place to stay in while there. At once they made arrangements to hold outdoor meetings every night, to their knowledge the first Seventh-day Adventist meetings held on Cayman Brac. At the end of their week's stay they left a little company of twelve people who were committed to keeping the Sabbath and meeting every week. Ross, in turn, gave his word he would send them a minister as soon as he returned to Jamaica. He was able to arrange with the committee to send Elder Frank Fletcher back to the island to carry on the work with these new believers. Because of a storm at sea and a disabled ship, the Adventist work was begun on Cayman Brac, and later a church was built there.

With repairs to the refugee ship made, she again set sail. After a restless night on board, Ross awoke and looked at his watch. It was 4:00 A.M. In just two hours they would be landing in a little cove near the small town of Black River, Jamaica. There in that bleak hour before dawn he thought of his predicament, and the more he thought about it, the more preposterous it seemed. Here he was, a minister of the gospel being smuggled illegally into a country! Like a criminal he had to cower in fear of the law. He groaned with frustration and despair when he visualized the headlines in the paper should he be apprehended: "President of Seventh-day Adventist Church in Jail for Illegal Entry." The thought that he might have inadvertently jeopardized the Lord's work caused a big knot to form in his stomach.

At first light the boat slipped quietly into the cove near Black River, and the passengers made their way into town singly or two by two so as not to attract attention. Ross and Sam walked in together and found a hotel, where they secured a room. They shut the door behind them and breathed a sigh of relief. Safe at last! The next day they would take the train to Kingston and home.

However, their relief was short lived, for soon they heard a knock on the door, and upon opening it they stood face to face with a policeman who greeted them with, "You are under arrest!"

Startled by this intrusion, Ross blurted out, "What have we done?"

"You've entered the country unauthorized. You must come with me to the jail and explain to the chief."

It was with some chagrin that Ross walked down the street in the custody of a police officer. Sam proved to be a true friend and never left him, so together they stood before the chief while Ross told his story. Fortunately the officer turned out to be sympathetic with his problem, and after checking around to verify Ross's identity, he released him.

The next day they were on their way to Kingston by train. Each click of the wheels seemed to be saying, "Going home, going home."

Ross opened the front door of his house and called out, "Anybody home?"

Gertrude scarcely recognized the gaunt, emaciated, sun-tanned man who stood before her. She had longed for him those long weeks of absence. And she had spent days and nights filled with worry and anxiety over Sonny Boy, who had contracted a serious illness shortly after Ross left. The little boy was getting better now, and Ross was home at last; and in her heart she thanked God for those blessings.

Chapter 20
A Good Seaman

Throughout his life Ross had noted a pattern in the significance of any year ending in eight, and he laughingly called it his magic number. As 1928 approached, the feeling stole over him that this was going to be a year of changes. He dismissed the impression and indeed forgot about it, but as the year rolled around events began to happen, good and bad, fortunate and unfortunate, of such importance that they either changed his thinking or were to be highly treasured in his memories.

In the first place, his career seemed to be gyrating wildly. At that time and for one reason and another there were many changes in the Inter-American Division. Several fields were looking for new presidents, and at the union conference Ross was elected president of Santo Domingo. Before he ever got to that field, however, he was asked to give it up and remain in Jamaica as president. Elder Edmed was going to replace Elder Hurdon, but it was necessary for him to remain in England for six months. Rather than leave Jamaica without a leader such a long time, Ross was asked to take over that position instead of going to Santo Domingo, and he agreed. At the same time the West Indian Training College in Jamaica was temporarily left without a president. Because Ross was the only man there with teaching experience, he was persuaded to take over this additional job.

The call to the Bahamas came suddenly and as a surprise. Ross had just begun to settle in to his new duties as conference president of Jamaica and as president of West Indian Training College, where he expected to remain for several years. However, that summer the Inter-American Division Council was held in Ancon, Canal Zone, and one more change was in the offing.

While Ross was there as one of the representatives from Jamaica, Elder Ogden, now head of the union conference, called him to his room for a private conference. He started talking hesitatingly like one who bears bad tidings. "Ross, don't be shocked and don't be hasty in making any decisions, but Harry Beddoe is here from Nassau looking for a man to head up the work in those islands, and . . ." He hesitated before plunging on. "And he has asked for you."

"For me!" Ross exclaimed, "This makes the fourth change I have had to consider in the last few months. Why me, of all people? There are plenty of capable men they could place there."

"Well, you see," Elder Ogden went on almost apologetically, "their great problem is that not every man they get can take the travel, which is entirely by sailboat. The last two men they had were so subject to seasickness they had to give up the work and return to the States. Your fame as a seaman has gotten around, and you are the one he wants."

Ross felt torn by this new and unexpected change in direction. Seeing his agitation, Elder Ogden said, "Don't answer me now. Let's pray about it and decide later."

In the afternoon of that same day, Harry Beddoe came to him and told of his predicament. "We have not been able to find one man who can sail without seasickness. Not one. They come all excited and full of enthusiasm, not only for the work there but the romance and adventure as well, but one trip on those seas in a small boat and they are done for. Now we all know you are a good sailor, Ross, so I hope you will consider the position."

"I have heard of many reasons for calling a man to a certain field, but this is the first time I ever knew of calling one because he is a good seaman," he said with a wry smile.

"You'll have to admit it is a valid reason. No matter who we get, he can't just sit in an office in Nassau and send out letters. He has to visit the territory."

"That is true," Ross replied, "and sailing is the only way to get from island to island. I love sailing. Just give me a small boat and a good breeze."

"Then you'll come?" Harry asked eagerly.

"I didn't say I would come; I said I love sailing. But I will give it some serious thought," Ross promised.

After some deliberation he and Gertrude decided it was a challenging call and one he should respond to. Consequently, in the summer of 1929 the Sypes landed in Nassau, where they rented a house in the suburbs. It was built to be hurricane proof because the owner had lost two houses in that place in previous storms. The walls were eighteen inches of reinforced cement, and the roof was bolted into the concrete walls. A new room was built on one side for the library and for a play room for the children, but it was not built for hurricanes. The need for a storm-proof building was not apparent to them until November 29 of that year, when the worst hurricane in the history of Nassau hit.

On Wednesday evening when it became apparent the storm was going to strike the island, Ross and Gertrude nailed boards over the windows, braced the doors, and tried to protect the garage as much as possible. The new addition containing their books and children's toys seemed ridiculously fragile now, so they carried some things out and barricaded the door. Feeling utterly cut off from everything and everyone, they huddled in the house lighted by a lamp and a flickering candle as the storm bore down. Rain beat against the doors and windows and flowed into the house in spite of their precautions. The wind howled in fury, sounding like myriad wild stampeding animals. The front door started to weaken under the onslaught, and the boards they had nailed across it cracked under the strain.

"Ross, the door!" shouted Gertrude above the roaring and creaking.

"What can I do?" he exclaimed. "There is nothing to fix it with." Then he remembered the table leaves stored out in the garage. Climbing out a side window and hugging the wall to keep from being blown away, he lugged the three table leaves in. Just as he got back inside there was a terrible sound of shattered wood as the garage collapsed on top of the car and was swept away. Since the windows were boarded over, they could see nothing, but above the sinister roar of the storm, they could hear buildings being ripped away and crashing in the street.

Because it remained in one spot for so long, this was to go down in the record books as one of the most unusual hurricanes ever to strike. Usually one of those storms will pass over in six to ten hours, but this one began with semihurricane force on Wednesday night, and lasted all day Thursday, not letting up until Friday morning. The wind reached a velocity of 185 miles per hour and then the instruments blew away, so the exact velocity was never known.

All Wednesday night and Thursday the wind raged on. In spite of the solid construction of the house it sounded at times as if the roof were being torn off. Then sometime Thursday there was a dead calm. The wind died down and the quiet was as terrifying as the sound and fury of the storm had been. The children ran to their parents to be held, and Gertrude said, "Oh, thank heaven, it is over at last. Come on, Ross, let's take these boards down." She was inclined to claustrophobia and hated the idea of being confined.

"No, don't touch the windows," Ross exclaimed. "The storm isn't over yet. You have heard of the eye of the hurricane, haven't you? This is it. It will come back from the other direction harder than ever in a little bit."

The storm wasn't over until sometime Friday when the wind abated and the sun came out. Ross and Gertrude went out to survey the damage and found the garage was gone and the car smashed, the library and play room blown away and books scattered everywhere. Ross and Harry Beddoe walked the two miles to the center of town, where the streets were flooded, houses torn down and scattered around, iron telephone poles twisted like tin and thrown across the streets. A large sailing vessel was lying across the main road, and small boats were stranded in unlikely places.

When they arrived at the church they found it had been completely demolished. Upon inquiring how the church members had fared, they were relieved to hear that none had been killed or even seriously injured, but many had lost their homes. One sister had a close call. She lived in a small house beside a larger one, and as the storm gathered strength, something told her to go to the big house. She dashed across the way, and when she looked back, saw to her horror the little house she had just left picked up by the wind and tumbled across the field.

For his first sermon after the storm Ross chose for his text Romans 8:28, "We know that all things work together for good to them that love God, to them who are the called according to his purpose." Those words seemed to be prophetic, for following the hurricane and the damage it left in its wake, the work went forward with new vigor. The colporteurs had better success than ever before. Not only was the church rebuilt, but a second church was built in a distant section of the island.

Ever since his love affair with sailing had begun, Ross had a secret longing for a boat of his own, and now that one would be so useful to his work, he began to hang around boat yards looking at boats. One of the men in his church in Nassau was a boat builder, so Ross hired him to build a boat to be used for missions and also for recreational sailing. The boat was only twenty-two feet long but was built to stand the high seas. It had a four-foot keel and into the keel was built a four-hundred-pound bar of iron to hold it in the water and make it difficult to capsize. The little craft had a thirty-five-foot mast and could travel at a good speed for a boat of its size, in addition to being very seaworthy. Ross named it after his young son, Sonny Boy, as he was affectionately called at that time.

One bright sparkling morning the *Sonny Boy* was sailing before a brisk breeze bound for the island of Eleuthera. Ross had a crew of two natives with the dignified names of Luke and Matthew. Luke, a small grizzled man with a crooked leg that gave him a truly nautical gait, was pleasant enough but he never smiled, never removed his cap, night or day, indoors or out, and never spoke a word he didn't have to. All of his love was centered on a small gray cat named Mousie he had smuggled on board. When the wind came up and the boat began to pitch, Luke ran frantically about to find Mousie and put her in a box fastened down in the galley. Whenever he caught a fish, which he prepared skillfully, he always saved the best morsels for Mousie.

Matthew was tall and handsome and full of good spirits and, like Ross, loved sailing. To be on the seas in a sailboat with the wind and the spray and the stars and the sun was to ask for nothing else. On the trip to Eleuthera, Matthew was at the wheel. The day was perfect for sailing. Brisk winds had been pushing them along, but as the sun began to drop into the sea there was no sign of land. Ross became uneasy as they had expected to reach the island before dark. "Are you sure you are on course?" he asked Matthew.

"Yes, I am positive," he answered, checking the instruments again and frowning in concentration. "Look, you can see for yourself."

"I don't understand it. We should be sighting land by now," Ross said, puzzled.

"Yes, sir, I know we should, Elder," replied Matthew, "but we ain't. Ain't no land in sight."

No sooner were these words out of his mouth than they struck a sand bar and came to a shuddering halt. Ross knew they were off course somehow, for they should have been in deep waters. They pushed away from the bar only to hit another a few rods away. When he checked the chart Ross found the only sand bar out of sight of land was fifty miles off their course. They were heading away from their goal to the southeast.

"Throw out the anchor, boys," he shouted, "we must get our bearings."

When he went to check the compass, he found there was a fishhook with a steel leader lying next to it. This had distorted the compass reading and turned them off course. They remained anchored all night, and next morning they were able to set their course and sail on to Eleuthera, a day late.

Examining the steel leader and the fishhook, Luke and Matthew marveled that such a little thing could take them so far off course. "That is like our conscience," Ross told them. "We must keep the conscience free from sin in order for it to be a safe guide. When sin is entertained, our compass ceases to guide us correctly."

Crooked Island had one of the largest churches in that field. It was, in fact, about the largest church of any kind on that island. The message asking Ross to come had been brought to them by Myra, a remarkable woman of unusual sweetness, intelligence, and depth of character. A native of Crooked Island, she had gone to Florida to work for a wealthy family, the Archers. Mrs. Archer gave her Bible studies, and her life changed. Myra accepted Jesus and began attending church. She seemed to become more beautiful in face and form, more regal in bearing, and more loving to others. One day she came to her employer and said, "I must go back to Crooked Island."

Mrs. Archer was stunned and asked, "What's wrong? Is someone sick? Do you want more money? Have we offended you?"

"No, no nothing like that," Myra was quick to reply. "In fact, it is because of your goodness that I must go."

"I don't understand," said Mrs. Archer.

"Don't you see," Myra explained, "you brought the story of Jesus to me, and now I must go back to Crooked Island and tell my people. No one has ever gone there with this message."

So she went back and found many looking for truth. Because of a schism in the established religion, the Church of England, many were spiritually disoriented and confused. This separation arose out of a conflict between the two rituals of that church, the high and the low. The people of Crooked Island were set against the high church ritual. When a new bishop came and they found they were now under a high church bishop, they rebelled. Many of the members went over to the Methodists or drifted into other churches. There was a lot of discontent when Myra arrived. With her high intelligence and natural gift for teaching and leadership, she began studies with a large number of interested men and women. Ross sailed over to the island to meet with the new believers and found himself in the midst of an interesting situation.

The Lord Bishop, hearing of this state of affairs—the waning membership and the drifting to other churches—came to Crooked Island to see if he could reclaim some of his former members. When told that most of them were now Seventh-day Adventists, he came prepared to tell them why they should keep Sunday. He was going to preach in his church on Sunday morning. Ross urged all of the former members to go and hear him. He told them, "We do not often have a Lord Bishop on this island, so I am urging you to attend this meeting. I shall be there as well, for I wish to know why they keep Sunday." He went on to tell them that since the Church of England had no lights in their church and could not hold a night meeting, he would hold a Sunday night meeting in the Adventist church, and if it seemed necessary he would review the bishop's sermon at that time.

On Sunday morning the church was filled with Seventh-day Adventists who had come to hear the Lord Bishop, splendid in his beautiful robe, and sitting on a sort of throne rigged up for him. Noble in appearance, awe-inspiring even, he spoke to them like a kindly potentate. "My children," he began, lifting beautiful white hands decorated with rings, "I am happy to be with you. I have promised to tell you why we keep Sunday as our rest day or the Lord's Day." He leaned forward earnestly, the white hair like a halo around the handsome face, the blue eyes mild. "When Jesus our Savior was born in Bethlehem of Judea the entire world was changed. All of the old laws and the Sabbaths were done away with, so from then on we have kept the first day of the week as our rest day." Then he went on to tell about the Resurrection being on Sunday. He did not read a single text of Scripture, nor did he have a Bible with him as he delivered his short sermon. The bishop's talk turned out to be fruitless as he attempted to persuade his old members.

That night Ross preached to a very large crowd and told them first of all that the Lord Bishop seemed to be a very fine and kindly gentleman, and he was impressed by his nondiscriminating spirit, for he had said nothing against the Seventh-day Adventists. "But as you know," Ross went on, "he did not read a single text of Scripture, and since he did not, he said nothing which I need reply to. So I will preach tonight on why I am a Seventh-day Adventist."

Chapter 21
Paul Ward

When Paul Ward first joined the Seventh-day Adventist Church, his wife would not cook for him anymore. "How can I cook without pig?" she wanted to know.

Paul's father told him, "You are no longer my son."

He had brought such shame upon his mother that she walked across the road to avoid meeting him and would not talk to him. Children threw rocks when he went by. One Sabbath morning his best friend stood waiting for him by the path leading to the church. When Paul appeared he took out a knife and threw it at a tree. Pulling it out, he drew his thumb gingerly along the sharp blade and glared at Paul. He said nothing.

Week after week Paul went to church, where a few members worshiped together. He was just an ordinary man whom you would pass on the street without noticing, not tall, not handsome, not gifted; but he exercised an implicit faith that is seldom seen. He became the local elder in the church on San Salvador, and gradually the church's membership increased. After some years this group included Paul's wife, his father, his mother, his best friend, and the children who threw rocks.

The island of San Salvador is the place where Christopher Columbus first landed in the New World. In 1930 there were three settlements, one on the southeast part, one on the west coast called Cockburn Town, and one on the north end called United Estates. A lake splits the island lengthwise and at that time served as a waterway between the towns. There were no roads and no vehicles on the island.

The people lived by barter, scarcely knowing what money was. Such products as they raised—corn, pigeon peas, yams, pigs, and goats—would be consumed by the farmers or perhaps traded for fish. There was one little shop with nothing in stock but flour, sugar, and soap, and even here there was no exchange of money. Business was conducted by barter, giving new or perhaps old meaning to the word *trade*. The people were entirely self-sufficient, not even buying salt, for they made their own from sea water.

One day a boat landed in Nassau, and the captain phoned Ross that he had some tithe for him from San Salvador. Driving down to get it, he found waiting for him at the dock a bag of pigeon peas and a young goat. He bought both for his own use and put the money in the church coffers. The pigeon peas the family subsequently ate, but the goat fared better, because Sonny Boy received it for a pet.

When it was time for the annual Week of Sacrifice offering, Ross did not write to San Salvador since he knew no one had money there. However, much to his surprise, he received a letter from Paul Ward containing five pounds in English money and a note saying the money was for the Week of Sacrifice offering. There was no further explanation, and Ross wondered how the islanders could raise that much money, for he was sure one could not find five pounds in the entire congregation. On his next trip to the island, he asked Paul where the five pounds came from.

"I knew you would wonder about that," he replied, "but I thought I would wait until you came here to tell you the story."

At prayer meeting on a Wednesday night, Paul had announced that the next week was the Week of Sacrifice offering. He had read about it in the church paper, and he told the congregation they should pray for money for this offering. But they all shook their heads dourly and reminded him there was no money on the island. He said to them, "God has some for us, so let's pray for Him to lead us to it." After the meeting Paul and his cousin, whom he always called Cousin Jimmy, went into the bush behind the church, and under the stars they prayed for the offering.

The next day, Thursday, the captain of a stranded boat showed up at Paul's house looking for men to help get his ship off the ground. The ship had been on its way from England to Australia by way of the Panama Canal. Steaming south in the main channel of sea travel that ran some miles east of the island, it got off course and ran aground on the north end of San Salvador. Since the ship was stuck fast and unable to move, it would be necessary to cast off some of its cargo, so the captain went ashore and asked where he could hire some men to help lighten the ship. He was told if he would go over to Cockburn Town and find Paul Ward, he could find some husky members of his church.

Paul got his crew together and helped the captain dislodge the boat. For this service they were paid five pounds. They knew this was the answer to their prayers, and as much as they needed the money, they sent the entire amount in for the sacrifice offering.

As he heard the story, Ross's eyes filled with tears. Missionaries were sent here to teach the natives, but these simple people were teaching others the true meaning of sacrifice.

One year the usual rains didn't come, and there was a terrible drought, especially bad on Cat Island and San Salvador. Ross took a trip with several cases of food to distribute. When he reached San Salvador he found Paul already at work handing out food to the distressed people. Ross asked him how he managed to help them all in this way. His reply was, "You know, Elder, these people threatened to kill me when I accepted this message, but now they are dependent on me for food. God has abundantly blessed me, and I am now able to help them in their distress." His great faith was inspiring to all, and Ross hailed him as a modern Joseph.

Ross had long felt a burden for Cat Island, but the evils of witchcraft enslaved the people there and made it hard to reach them with the gospel. One day, two of the brethren in Nassau, Ethan and Dan, who were part-time colporteurs, came to his office. Ethan said, "Elder Sype, we want to go to Cat Island and take the gospel to those poor souls."

"Cat Island?" Ross questioned in surprise, for these were not experienced men. "You know of the problem over there with witchcraft?"

"We know," answered Dan, "but we want to go. We heard you say we should begin work out there sometime—no one has gone, and we want to go."

Seeing their determination, Ross agreed to supply them with Bibles and books and to pay their passage over. They set forth firm in their belief, resolving to do what no one else had ever done—bring the gospel to Cat Island. Many stories of witchcraft and evil had been borne from that narrow, low-lying island. In spite of the great mystery that hung over the place, Ethan and

Dan caught a boat going to Cat Island. They felt some apprehension as they watched the outline of the island come into view. Then as they disembarked and stood on the lonely dock watching the boat pull away without them, the hard cold fact faced them that they would have to remain here until some vessel happened by. Sullen native people watched them carry their books and belongings ashore, but no one offered help.

Undaunted, they set to work at once, walking for miles and knocking on doors, only to be met by people ranging from unfriendly to hostile. No one would buy anything or even talk to them. One and all refused the free literature until one day they stopped at a cottage and found a small group of women gathered around in the yard studying a book. For the first time since their arrival at Cat Island, the two men found curious and friendly faces turned toward them as they introduced their work. The book the women had been reading turned out to be an Adventist publication one of them had received on board a sailing vessel. She and her friends had been studying together, puzzling over the things they read. Now in answer to their prayer for understanding, help had come. They gathered around Ethan and Dan full of questions.

The lady of the house asked the canvassers to stay for supper and spend the night so they would be able to talk with her husband. Like his wife, he became interested in the message and requested studies for his family. This opening led to other contacts, and soon a little group was meeting regularly. In a few weeks Ross received a letter from Ethan and Dan asking him to come over and hold meetings in the village. The meetings were well attended and many accepted the truth, but others were fearful, held in the drag net of superstition. Some were openly hostile to religion.

Besides conducting meetings, Ross visited among the native people. One day he noticed a little island just off the shore of the main island. A well-worn path led to the small islet, so he decided to go over there and get acquainted. He found three or four houses clustered on this spit of land. Stopping at the first one, he knocked at the door. To his astonishment it was jerked open, revealing a woman with a club. Tall and broad and full of rage, she looked quite capable of using her weapon. "Get off this island!" she shouted. "We don't want to hear anything you have to say. We know all about you and your kind."

Ross backed away from the door and left, convinced that she would start clubbing him if she had a chance. He continued to hold meetings on the main island, and more and more men and women became interested in Jesus. Then he was called to go over to Long Island to dedicate a church, but he hated to leave Cat Island at this stage, so he sent word to Paul Ward to come over and work with the people while he was away. He told Paul about the angry woman.

Not one to be defeated, Paul went over and found the woman's husband, a fisherman. Paul asked him if he could go fishing with him. The fisherman was glad for the company, and they went several miles out to sea and remained all night, fishing and talking. There in the small boat on the great sea under the stars they talked of many things through the long watches of the night. As so often happens when people get into conversation, the discussion turned to faith and the Bible.

When the man returned home to his wife—the woman who had threatened Ross with a club—she asked him how the two men had gotten along with fishing.

He replied, "The fishing was good, but more important, this man told me a story about Jesus. When He invited some fishermen to follow Him and become disciples, He told them, 'I will make you fishers of men.' That's what Paul Ward is, a fisher of men. I'm going to join him at his meetings, and I hope you will too."

She sputtered at first, angry and protesting. Paul let her say what she had to say and then took his Bible out and began to read. "Come unto me, all ye that labour and are heavy laden, and I will give you rest" (Matthew 11:28). She listened, at first reluctantly, standing by the door, but as he read on, she edged closer and sat down by her husband. In her own hard life she recognized what it meant to labor and bear heavy burdens. Paul closed the Bible and prayed for God's blessing on this household. When he paused at the door to ask if they would like him to come and study with them, she shrugged and gave a little nod.

When Ross returned to the island after a few weeks, the fisherman and his wife were at church. She was standing at the door greeting people, with a Bible in her hand, not a club. Upon seeing the minister she ran to meet him, threw her arms around him saying, "Oh, Elder, and to think I was going to club you! I want to be baptized!"

Chapter 22
Farewell to the Islands

During the dark years of the Great Depression, the mission field grew and developed, and there was an increasing need for money. Since Ross's salary barely met the family needs, there seemed to be no way they could raise an extra cent to contribute to development. One day when Gertrude was reading the local paper, she noticed the names of all the celebrities who came to Nassau from the mainland in the winter months. A light went on in her mind, and she realized how she could raise money and help out. Before they had come to the mission field, she worked as a nurse and found she had a special talent as a masseuse. So a great idea was born. She had the talent and experience as a masseuse, and here was the market.

Since she was friendly and outgoing and skilled at her work, Gertrude soon had a good practice that included many of the rich and famous, people she had only read about before. Among her clientele were such well-known people as American movie star Gloria Swanson; Mrs. J. P. Morgan, wife of the well-known international financier; and Mrs. Andrew Mellon, whose husband was Secretary of the Treasury under presidents Harding, Coolidge, and Hoover. But best remembered was Winston Churchill, the powerful British statesman. He had been in an automobile accident while in New York and had come to Nassau to recuperate. Gertrude was recommended to him for hydrotherapy and massage treatments. In the three weeks she took care of him they had some inspiring visits, and when he left he gave her a recommendation stating that in her hands were "both power and virtue." In this way she was able to raise money to help in the building of several churches on the outlying islands.

After years of serving in remote, far-flung islands, Ross found he was extending himself beyond his strength, and when the tide turned, there seemed no way of stopping it. One misadventure followed another; illness came upon illness, until it seemed as if the islands themselves were telling him to let go—leave it all behind and go home to the United States.

The Sype house in Nassau was perched high on a hill with a sweeping view of the harbor, where the tall masts of ships could be seen from a great distance. Ross often took a mail boat out to the other islands, and when it was time for his return, Minita and Sonny Boy stood on the front steps gazing as far down the harbor channel to the right as they could see. Each tried to be the first to sight the boat and shout out, "Here he comes!" When it sailed into view, they called their mother, and all watched as the little craft bringing Daddy home drew nearer and sailed smoothly past them, heading for the wharf. In a frenzy to be off then, they trooped out to the car and sped down to meet the boat.

They knew Ross would be out on deck, waving, ready to leap ashore as soon as the boat docked. But one day in 1934 when they met the boat, he was not there waving from the deck, and he didn't come striding briskly down the gangplank. In fact, he was nowhere to be seen. "Where is Daddy?" asked the children. Gertrude looked anxiously up and down and was about to go on board when she saw him. But could that really be Ross? Instead of bounding out to meet them, he was lying on a homemade stretcher carried by two strong sailors.

"Ross," she shouted, "what is wrong?"

"Sorry, ma'am," said one of the men, "he took sick on the way back. Must have been something he ate. Some of the crew is sick too."

Ross didn't have strength to stand by himself, so they helped him into the car, and Gertrude drove directly to the doctor. He was diagnosed as having food poisoning. She took him home and nursed him back to health, but he never regained his former strength and verve.

When Ross was able to return to work, one of his first visits was to Long Island. While there he met with another mishap. He was riding a horse from one meeting place to another. The little animal, picking its way along a rocky path, stepped into a hole and fell, throwing Ross off its back. He landed heavily, striking his head on a rock, and lay there for some time before regaining consciousness. Sitting up, he rubbed his head and discovered a lump that throbbed painfully. Although dizzy and weak, he staggered over to the horse, grazing nearby, and somehow managed to mount and continue on. The next day he ached all over and was hardly able to get out of bed. He gradually recovered from this misfortune but did not return to his former strength.

Gertrude and the children had gone to Florida to visit Ross's parents when the last blow fell. Ross was again visiting the outlying islands on a small mail boat. All went well until the return trip. He had worked hard, putting in long days holding meetings, visiting, baptizing, and counseling. On the return trip aboard the boat, he felt utterly exhausted as he flung himself on his bunk, not having the strength to make it up on deck, where he usually enjoyed the scenery and activity. He fell asleep and then tried to leave his bunk, perhaps to go to the restroom, but didn't make it any farther than the door, where he blacked out. Much later a ship's officer found him crumpled on the floor, unconscious. The men cared for him the best they could on board the small, unequipped vessel. When the boat docked in Nassau, a conference officer came and took Ross to his home and cabled Gertrude.

Gertrude rushed back to Nassau. She could tell Ross needed more medical help than he could obtain on the islands, so she immediately booked passage for Miami. From there she drove him to his mother and stepfather's home near Orlando and placed him under the care of a specialist for several weeks. The doctor told him that he was in no condition to return to the islands and advised him to remain in the States, as it would take a long time for his body to rebuild itself.

So for the last time the family went back to the islands, this time to pack up their belongings and leave. So many memories had accumulated there; it was hard to say goodbye. A worker drove them down to the dock in the old Essex that had served them so well. With the missionary years behind them, they boarded a boat headed for Florida and America, where new adventure and further years of service in ministerial work awaited them.

Epilogue

After returning to the United States permanently, Ross and Gertrude spent many years in ministerial and chaplain work in the South, Northwest, and for a short time, Canada. They remained active well into their eighties, when Ross retired from his position as chaplain of Walker Memorial Hospital in Avon Park, Florida, and Gertrude from private duty nursing.

When they could no longer maintain their home, the Sypes went to live with their daughter Minita and son-in-law Glenn. Their son Jack—Sonny Boy in the story—and his wife, Alta, lived nearby.

They enjoyed listening to Minita read to them portions of this book when it was in progress, reliving the old days in the mission field when they were on the cutting edge, bringing the Word of God to the dear souls in the islands.

Living with Minita on a Florida key, Ross loved to sit in the yard under the coconut palms, watching the boats pass by—especially the graceful sailboats. His thoughts went back to the Caribbean, where he sailed the *Sonny Boy,* sails bending before a stiff breeze, the vast sea before him.

Gertrude enjoyed living on the Keys, but she never forgot Iowa where her roots were and returned often to visit. She and her brothers and sisters were healthy and robust into their eighties, still enjoying a good meal and a good story and never without a certain dry sense of humor, a witty phrase at the ready. In their eighties, three of them, brother Merle Hunt, sister Georgia Coy, and Gertrude drove the sixty miles up to a family reunion one summer day. When they were walking back to their car to leave, one of the nephews said to his brothers and sisters, "Take a good look, kids, and never you forget it, that's the kind of stock you came from."

God put these two faithful workers, the intrepid gringo and his loyal companion, to rest before this book was finished. Gertrude died at ninety-two in 1982 and Ross at ninety-four-and-a-half in 1984. They rest from their labors and await the call of the Life-Giver.

If you enjoyed this book,
you'll enjoy these as well: